Saving the
Savings and Loan

Saving the Savings and Loan

THE U.S. THRIFT INDUSTRY AND THE TEXAS EXPERIENCE, 1950–1988

M. Manfred Fabritius
and
William Borges

PRAEGER

New York
Westport, Connecticut
London

Library of Congress Cataloging-in-Publication Data

Fabritius, M. Manfred.
    Saving the savings and loan.

    Bibliography: p.
    Includes index.
    1. Building and loan associations—Texas—History—
20th century.   2. Building and loan associations—
United States—History—20th century.   I. Borges,
William.   II. Title.
HG2153.T4F33   1989   332.3′2′09764   88-32942
ISBN 0-275-93161-7 (alk. paper)

Library of Congress Catalog Card Number: 88-32942
ISBN: 0–275–93161–7

First published in 1989

Praeger Publishers, One Madison Avenue, New York, NY 10010
A division of Greenwood Press, Inc.

Printed in the United States of America

The paper used in this book complies with the Permanent
Paper Standard issued by the National Information Standards
Organization (Z39.48-1984).

10   9   8   7   6   5   4   3   2   1

Contents

Illustrations

MAP

Abbreviations

ADC	acquisition, development, and construction
ARMs	Adjustable Rate Mortgages
ATs	Automatic Transfer Accounts
DIA	Depository Institutions Amendments
DIDC	Depository Institutions Deregulation Committee
DIDMCA	Depository Institutions Deregulation and Monetary Control Act
ECOA	Equal Credit Opportunity Act
ERISA	Employee Retirement Income Security Act
Fed	Federal Reserve Board
FDIC	Federal Deposit Insurance Corporation
FHA	Federal Housing Administration
FHLBs	Federal Home Loan Banks
FHLBB	Federal Home Loan Bank Board
FHLMC	Federal Home Loan Mortgage Corporation (Freddie Mac)
FIA	Financial Institutions Act

FIR	Federal Insurance Reserve
FNMA	Federal National Mortgage Association (Fannie Mae)
FSLIC	Federal Savings and Loan Insurance Corporation
GAAP	generally accepted accounting practices
GNP	gross national product
HCDA	Housing and Community Development Act
HOLC	Home Owners Loan Corporation
HUD	Department of Housing and Urban Development
IRA	Individual Retirement Account
MMC	money market certificate
NOW	Negotiable Order of Withdrawal account
NWC	net worth certificate
OMB	Office of Management and Budget
RAP	regulatory accounting practices
RESPA	Real Estate Settlement Procedures Act
S & L	savings and loan
S & Ls	savings and loans
VA	Veterans Administration
VRM	variable-rate mortgage

Acknowledgments

It is our pleasure to acknowledge the help and cooperation we have received in the preparation of this book. A general expression of thanks goes to the faculty members in the schools of business at the University of Mary Hardin-Baylor and Southwestern University. We appreciate the assistance and advice of our colleagues throughout the project's development.

We would also like to thank the many members of the savings and loan industry who, throughout our search for data, were so generous with their time and advice. In this regard we especially wish to thank Jack Cashin and Art Leiser, whose help was invaluable toward completing this project.

Another group to whom we are appreciative for their guidance, particularly in the editing stage, include Joseph Ewers, Forest Hill, and Walt Rostow.

Lastly we especially wish to thank Kathy Buchhorn who typed the manuscript and was so generous with her time.

1

Introduction

Notwithstanding the generally healthy business and economic climate of the United States in the 1980s, the nation's thrift industry[1] experienced two severe financial crises during the decade. In particular, the nation's savings and loan (S & L) industry faced problems of unprecedented enormity. In 1980 alone, the industry lost nearly $3 billion, when net income (after taxes) for all S & L associations dropped to $.8 billion, from its 1979 level of $3.7 billion.[2]

By 1981 things worsened as the industry suffered terribly, reporting a net loss of over $4 billion. This represented a negative return on assets of .75 percent.[3] Equally unsettling within the S & L industry was the closure of individual institutions as a result of industry-wide calamity. Indeed, by early 1982 thrift institutions were disappearing at the rate of one per day, meaning that nearly 10 percent of all S & Ls were closed in 1982 alone. Often these shutdowns were the result of unavoidable takeovers (generally on humiliating terms), but many institutions simply failed.[4] Finally, by May 1982, the Federal Home

Loan Bank Board (FHLBB) reported that the net worth of the 3,637 U.S. insured savings and loan (S & L) associations had declined for the seventeenth consecutive month.[5] This was the start of the first of two crises the S & L industry encountered in the 1980s.

THE PURPOSE OF THIS BOOK

An understanding of the contemporary S & L industry in the United States requires a familiarity with the history of the industry, as it is this history that reveals, to some extent, the current situation of S & Ls. Moreover, attention to historical detail provides insights about the legal, political, and social events that have shaped the modern S & L industry.

Throughout their history, U.S. S & Ls (savings and loans) have functioned as institutions with a single, primary purpose: financing the purchase and construction of homes for families of middle (i.e., median) income. To be sure, the history of this enterprise is inextricably tied to the reality of home ownership, over a period of decades, by the nation's nonrich. Indeed, when former FHLBB Chairman Edwin Gray remarked that home ownership is "part and parcel with the American dream, [as] it gives millions of Americans a stake in the system . . . and represents a cornerstone to the family, the neighborhood and the community,"[6] he reflected the popular view—that S & Ls commonly provide the vehicle for the realization of these traditional American values.

Significant to note is that, while the first century or so of S & L activity was restricted almost exclusively to the aggregation of savings for the purpose of home financing (that is, lending money to encourage homebuilding), considerable change has occurred within the industry, particularly since the end of World War II. Today the S & L industry is greatly diversified, engaging in such notable enterprises as home improvement loans, commercial real estate loans, consumer loans, investment in securities, educational loans, service corporations, credit cards, trust services, and others.[7] Therefore, it is no longer accurate to label S & Ls as merely financial agents of home ownership, though this remains the industry's central concern.

Mindful of the importance of the history and change among S & Ls, this book will constitute a study of the S & L industry, emphasizing to some extent Texas' role in transforming S & Ls from financers of home mortgages to multipurpose financial entities. The study's prime focus is the period 1950–88, selected because it represents the industry's most recent period of dramatic growth. Of equal importance is the fact that the decade of the 1950s, as is demonstrated, laid much of the foundation for the aforementioned industry-wide crisis of the 1980s. During that decade of rapid S & L growth, government regulations constrained the liability structure of the industry to short-term obligtions. In addition, tax laws favored a long-term asset structure. Thus the mismatching of asset and liability maturity was, by the end of the 1950s, firmly rooted in the U.S. S & L industry.

The purpose of this book is not only to chronicle the response of the national S & L industry to various laws, economic conditions, and changing times, but also to demonstrate how, in Texas, state-chartered S & Ls provided a model of S & L reform, one that reshaped not only the Texas S & L industry but the national industry as well. Moreover, as we shall see, some of the innovative reform demonstrated by Texas institutions caused problems of enormous magnitude—problems from which many S & Ls simply could not recover.

Still, the model for reform provided by Texas served an important function, as the industry needed help. This model came not only from within the state's S & L industry, but it was, in part, from Texas' regulatory provisions—which govern S & L behavior. Nationally, all S & L institutions with federal charters are bound by FHLBB rules. However, state-chartered associations are regulated by their individual state agencies.[8] When, as in the case of Texas, state regulations are less restrictive of S & L activity, it is helpful to compare behavior among the nation's institutions, in order to discern the impact of varying statutory provisions on their behavior, and to examine the relative measures of success enjoyed by the differently chartered S & Ls.

Interestingly enough Texas, like California, established regulatory policies that, across the board, were designed to permit S & L innovation. Indeed, both states have taken the lead in many other areas of enterprise, throughout their respective histories. What is noteworthy is the attention gained, particularly by Texas, following the federal move to deregulate. Such attention, according to no less an authority than Linton Bowmen, former commissioner of the Texas Savings and Loan Department, resulted in specific policies adopted by the federal government in the radically deregulatory Garn-St. Germain Act of 1982. In drafting the legislative measure, Bowmen notes, members of Congress copied policies and procedures already established among Texas state-chartered S & Ls.[9]

STRUCTURE AND ORGANIZATION

This book provides a chronological sequence of developments in the national and Texas S & L industries. To this end, the historical treatment is divided among five of the study's chapters, with greatest focus on recent S & L problems. To avoid arbitrariness, the chapters were not structured so as to include coverage of equal time periods; rather the division was made on the basis of characteristics that set each time period apart from others.

The first historical chapter provides an overview of national S & L activity. This chapter examines the inception of the S & L industry in the middle of the nineteenth century and briefly explores the early phases of S & L development. Then it chronicles the problems common to most financial institutions during the 1920s and follow-up years of the Great Depression, and concludes with a discussion of the post–World War II S & L boom.

Chapter 3 deals extensively with the 1950s U.S. housing "explosion" and covers the period of time until 1965 (the final year, for some time to come, of relatively low inflation and low interest rates). This period is of critical importance to the industry, as it was characterized by a stable national expansion of S & Ls and a simultaneous expansion of Texas S & Ls.

Chapter 4 examines the period 1966–78, an era characterized by irregular price movements and unpredictable inflation. Significantly, the chapter concludes with the very year prior to the start of a major crisis in the national S & L industry. Moreover, during this era Texas S & Ls set the stage for national innovation, as their concepts and practices were, to a great extent, incorporated into national legislation passed in 1980 and beyond.

Chapter 5, covering the years 1979–82, details the period of financial crisis weathered by the S & L industry. It explores the foreclosures, insolvency, and forced mergers that marked the era. Finally, it reveals information about a time in Texas' S & L history during which national attention focused on a few unscrupulous individuals operating in the state's industry.

The final historical chapter analyzes the period 1983–88. The 1983–86 period of nationwide S & L recovery is further characterized by a continuation of mergers. The last section of the chapter examines the 1986–88 period in which the second crisis of the decade occurred. The emphasis in this section is on alternative policies that offer the industry possible solutions to their grave problems.

The concluding chapter recaps the current plight of the national S & L industry. It attempts to isolate and assess the magnitude of the industry's remaining problems and to pinpoint possible future problems of which the industry need be conscious.

NOTES

1. Students of economics and finance typically employ the characterization "thrift industry" when referring to savings and loan institutions, mutual savings banks, finance companies, and other financial lending institutions. Throughout this book the term refers only to savings and loan institutions and mutual savings banks, as this more restrictive definition from Gail E. Makinen in *Money, Banking and Economic Activity* (New York: Academic Press, 1981), seems best-suited to the contemporary world of finance, and to this book.

2. *1982 Savings and Loan Source Book* (Chicago: United States League of Savings Associations, 1982), p. 40. Net income after taxes is computed by subtracting operating income from operating expense, which equals net operating income. This net operating income figure is then

taxed at current tax rates, which provides the net after-tax income figure.

3. Richard Pratt, "Office of the Chairman," *Federal Home Loan Bank Board—1981 Annual Report*, April 1982, p. 6.

4. Charles M. Weiser, "Texas Savings and Loan Branching," Professional Report, The University of Texas, December 1984, p. 1.

5. "Some Glimmers of Hope," *Standard & Poor's Industry Surveys 1983* (Standard & Poor's Corporation), p. 827.

6. Edwin J. Gray, "Matching Asset and Liabilities in a Thrift Portfolio," *Federal Home Loan Board Journal*, September 1983, p. 3.

7. U.S. Congress, *The Depository Institutions Deregulatory and Monetary Control Act of 1980*, Sec. 401.

8. It is not uncommon to find state regulatory agencies whose rules parallel those established by federal agencies.

9. Interview with Linton Bowmen, Texas Savings and Loan Department, Austin, February 15, 1986.

2

Early U.S. Banking and the Emergence of S & Ls

To millions of Americans concerned about the current S & L industry crisis, the near future, rather than the distant past, commands greatest attention. In view of the alarming possibilities—loss of public confidence, an unprecedented wave of S & L foreclosures, and a severe shortage of Federal Savings and Loan Insurance Corporation bail-out funds—facing thrifts, this is not surprising. But confronting the crisis seriously requires a realistic appraisal of the facts and events that preceded it; and these include several key episodes in the nation's 200-year history.

In this chapter we offer an overview of the U.S. banking and S & L history, pinpointing trends and occurrences of critical importance. Why survey banking history? Because, inasmuch as the S & L industry has its roots in banking, the long-standing problems of both bear more than a little resemblance. Moreover, the laws and regulations governing S & Ls stem from the long history of banking legislation. Therefore, despite the fact that S & Ls are commonly, and accurately, described as "specialty" institutions (centered around the needs of potential homeowners), their record cannot be viewed apart from that of their full-service banking competitors.

Here we begin with a brief examination of early U.S. banking as that industry's struggles paralleled those of our new government. This is followed by a review of the founding of the S & L industry, its early years, and long-standing objectives of industry officials. Included in this section is a discussion of the legal and regulatory restrictions that, historically, have constrained these officials.

The chapter continues with a look at how the nation's Great Depression impacted the S & L industry, in Texas and nationwide, and, equally important, how the industry responded to this crisis of unprecedented magnitude. Finally, we survey the range of national S & L activity in the postdepression years. This includes an examination of the development of the dual system of charters (of great significance in the decades to follow, as discussed in subsequent chapters) and the industry's experience during and in the immediate aftermath of World War II.

A final point deserves mention here. As scholars attempt to recreate history, they tend to impose upon it more merit than is warranted. In reality, most of our nation's history is better described as chaotic than orderly. Nevertheless, the practice of neatly compartmentalizing important trends and events persists and must be recognized—at least as a fact of academic life. Indeed, as we chronicle nearly two centuries of U.S. history in this chapter, we are guilty of bypassing much chaos and reaching for much order. Still, we have tried in earnest not to dismiss pertinent facts or trends in our account of this history.

EARLY U.S. BANKING

The structure and day-to-day operations of U.S. S & Ls have been shaped by the long, uneven history of the nation's banks, which are rooted in the earliest years of the republic. Thus, in order to understand the modern ties between U.S. financial institutions and governments (national and state), it is essential to recognize the key facts and events that accounted for their initial bond.

With virtually no exceptions, public or private, banks and

other financial institutions are the most closely monitored and regulated enterprises in the United States. In so controlling these institutions the national and state governments—particularly the former—find their authority in the U.S. Constitution. To be sure, since its ratification in 1789, presidents, sessions of Congress, and the Supreme Court have relied on the all-important document to justify a myriad of laws, regulations, and directives affecting the nation's financial institutions. Of equal significance, given the decentralized nature of both the banking and thrift industries, it is important to note state-to-state variations in laws and practices, as we proceed to do.

The power of Congress to regulate banking and other financial enterprises is found in Article I of the U.S. Constitution. Therein it is granted the power to make all laws "necessary and proper" to carry out its functions, as well as those of the other departments—executive and judicial—of the national government.[1] Additionally, Article I grants Congress the power to regulate commerce, in what is commonly referred to as the document's "commerce clause."[2] Broad Supreme Court interpretations of these two clauses have, over the span of two centuries, established the supremacy of the national legislature in matters related to finance (and, more broadly, to the national economy).

While the Constitution itself contains no references to banking per se, Congress, relying on the aforement authority bestowed upon it via the nation's highest court, has passed thousands of pieces of legislation that, collectively, govern the banking and thrift industries. Most significantly, Congress, in 1863 and 1864, passed banking acts creating the National Banking System; these acts, sanctioned by the Supreme Court, specifically authorized congressional regulation of financial institutions.

Besides Congress, other agencies of government, most notably the Federal Reserve System, have adopted laws and regulations that provide legal direction for U.S. banks and S & Ls. Finally, the 50 states—which, along with the national government, enjoy considerable regulatory power[3]—have created individual legal environments for their financial institutions and, as we shall see, these vary tremendously.

Though the future of U.S. banks and S & Ls is at the moment uncertain, two things are sure to hold constant: (1) Congress will continue to reign supreme over the states in all matters regarding the activities of financial institutions, whether they be chartered by the states or by the national government; and (2) the Supreme Court will continue to review specific acts of Congress, and of the states, to determine their constitutionality. This certainty rests on the strong likelihood that two long-standing decisions of the Supreme Court will not be overturned.

The first of these decisions stemmed from the 1803 case *Marbury v. Madison*, in which the Court established the principle of "judicial review." This gives the high court final authority in determining the constitutionality of any law passed by Congress, or by any of the states.[4] The second emerged from the critically important case *McCullouch v. Maryland*, wherein it was held that a state could not tax a national bank,[5] thus establishing the independence of these banks (and, more generally, the protection of one government from taxation levied by another government). Together, these rulings provide the basis for national supremacy over the states in the governance of banks and S & Ls.

The first act of Congress to have a direct bearing on national banking occurred in 1791, with the chartering of the First Bank of the United States. At the time, many bankers, lawyers, and statesmen believed that the charter stood in violation of the two-year-old Constitution, inasmuch as it contained no specific provision authorizing Congress such power. Later, following the determination that the act was in accordance with the law of the land, many came to assume that Congress possessed the authority to act however it chooses as long as it does not violate the Constitution's specific provisions or its explicit objectives.[6] This view has come to dominate constitutional debate, primarily because it has been fostered repeatedly by the Supreme Court.

Notwithstanding these early victories by the national government, states dominated early U.S. banking. This was due mainly to the provincial, decentralized character of the early United States. Thus even though the foundation for a national banking system was laid early, it would not become a reality until 1864, following passage of the aforementioned banking acts. It was only then that Congress moved to furnish the United States with a uniform paper currency, replacing the variegated note issues of some 1,600 state-chartered banks.[7] This also resulted in creation of the so-called dual banking system, still in existence.

The dual system has, for more than a century now, enabled banks to operate under either a federal or state charter. Consequently, a "dual" precedent was created for other financial institutions, including S & Ls. Because rules, regulations, and laws vary among the states, a series of problems faces the national government wherever it seeks to address issues concerning the financial intermediaries industry. Oftentimes, the solution to a problem facing the thrift industry in one state has little bearing on its counterparts in other parts of the country. Indeed, much of this book is devoted to an account of the national government's struggle to bring order, stability, and fiscal soundness to 50 somewhat independent thrift industries.

Later in this volume we make reference to additional federal statutes of significance, and we consider the possible consequences of each. These include the acts creating the Federal Reserve System in 1913, the Federal Home Loan Bank Board in 1932, and the Federal Deposit Insurance Corporation in 1933. In addition, we focus on the 1933 Homeowners Loan Act, the 1980 Depository Institutions Deregulation and Monetary Control Act, and the 1982 Garn–St. Germain Depository Institutions Act, as well as several rules enacted in recent years by the Federal Home Loan Bank Board. The impact of these laws and rulings on modern S & Ls is significant and essential to an understanding of the plight of this embattled industry.

THE FOUNDING OF THE SAVINGS AND LOAN INDUSTRY

The earliest U.S. ancestors of today's S & Ls were called building and loan associations.[8] These were established for the sole purpose of solving the problem of home financing. Similar institutions had existed in England since the eighteenth century, part of what were termed "building societies." The first such society, established in Birmingham in 1781, was followed by several others (often referred to as "British associations"). In describing the cause behind the establishment of these institutions, Jack Cashin suggested that they were "the means whereby the industrial classes of Great Britain have supplied their economic needs for themselves, no man showing them the way, not by prescription nor by influence of superiors."[9] It was this yearning for independence and success that propelled early Americans, half a century later, to begin building their nation's S & L industry.

During the first 50 years of the existence of the United States as a nation, its population increased fourfold, creating a sharp rise in housing needs. This spurred creation of the nation's first building and loan association, which addressed the problem of housing shortages in the country's major commercial and industrial communities.

In addition to the housing shortage problem, workers, by the 1820s and 1830s, had become less inclined to build their own houses. As their wages grew, more and more laborers—especially those employed in factories—had less incentive and less time to undertake such an ambitious task. Moreover, with the rapid growth of cities, materials grew scarce and more costly.

So the typical early-nineteenth-century American, though financially capable of buying a home, was disinclined to be his own architect, financier, and builder; for these jobs he needed help, and this required credit, as few were able to accumulate capital sufficient to pay cash for a home. However, banks were initially unwilling to finance homebuilding, and potential buyers were moved to seek other, collective means of facilitating their home purchases. Consequently, English settlers, already familiar with British building societies, used their knowledge to establish nearly identical U.S. enterprises.

The first building and loan association in the United States was established in Frankford, Pennsylvania, a small factory town, in 1831.[10] As new settlers arrived to work in the town's textile and tanning mills, they needed houses. Then, as they became wage earners, they came to demand housing, and their building and loan association would make such housing possible.

Indeed, the first Oxford Provident[11] was created less than a year after it was proposed. Its constitution stated that the specialized organization was formed solely "to contributors thereof to build or purchase dwelling houses."[12] Thereafter, it held, remaining funds were to be divided among their members, after which time the association would be terminated.

The corporate body of the Oxford Provident, like those of its English forerunners, was composed of members who enjoyed mutual ownership and management of the association. Each member was required to attend monthly meetings and to participate—through discussion, voting on a wide range of issues, and election of the board of trustees—in the association's decision-making process.[13] Operations were patterned after those of the Birmingham Building Society. As such, its funds came solely from membership dues, including fines for delinquencies in payment of dues.[14]

The Oxford Provident was managed by 13 trustees, elected from the members, to serve one-year terms. These trustees supervised all operations, and their jobs ranged from providing financial advice to examining land and titles. However, for none of these services did any trustee receive direct or indirect compensation.[15]

Because each member was guaranteed a loan, there were no provisions for other withdrawals. The means by which an individual could recover his investment prior to the organization's termination was by leaving the association. In most cases members remained, and upon accumulation of sufficient capital the trustees would announce that the association was prepared to advance a sum. Members would bid on premiums to be paid for such advances, and loans would go to those offering the highest bids.[16] But conditions of the loans were clear and strict. Each was to be used solely for "the purpose of erecting a dwelling or purchasing one (within an area not more) than five miles from the market house in the Borough of Frankford (and not outside of) the county of Philadelphia."[17]

The process of bidding each time the association's fund reached an adequate sum ($500) continued until every member had secured a loan. The Oxford Provident, which succeeded, eventually, in making possible the purchase or construction of homes for all of its members who so desired, finally was dissolved in 1841, ten years after its creation.[18]

SAVINGS AND LOAN GROWTH: THE TEXAS STORY

News of the success of the Oxford Provident spread rapidly. As its ongoing accomplishments became clear, people in neighboring towns formed similar organizations. Thus by 1840 there were, in Philadelphia alone, more than 50 building and loan associations.[19]

Eventually, news of the Frankford organization reached distant communities. Then, as the population increased and began moving westward, the demand for building and loan associations increased. On Map 1,[20] dates corresponding to the establishment of each state's first building and loan association reflect the movement's rapid spread, particularly in the mid-nineteenth century. Generally, the dates correspond well with the major population movements and settlement concentrations of last century.

Table 2.1 denotes the estimates of the worth of the industry, compiled by U.S. Commissioner of Labor Carroll D. Wright in 1893. The industry's growth over the succeeding 60 years is shown in Table 2.2. Here we see that S & L growth—greatest during the 1920s—was fairly steady through the immediate post–World War II era.

As the S & L industry moved westward—from Pennsylvania to Kentucky, and then to Tennessee—the state of Texas was destined to enjoy its offerings. But it was not until after the close of the Civil War, in 1866, that Texas chartered its first corporate S & L, when the state legislature approved establishment of the Young Men's Mutual Real Estate and Building Association.[21] This association began with $60,000 in capital stock, which was divided into 100 shares (at $600 per share), payable in monthly installments of $10.[22]

By modern standards the Young Men's Mutual Real Estate and Building Association of Houston could hardly be considered an S & L; it more closely resembled a modern real es-

Map 1.
Date of the First Building and Loan Activity in Each State

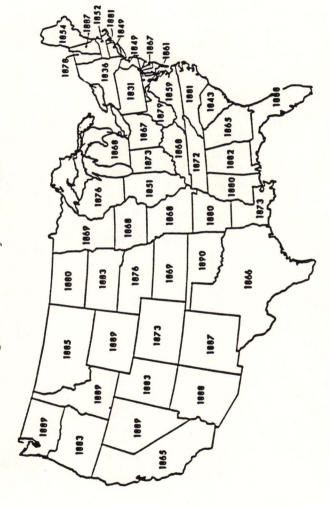

Source: H. Morton Bodfish: *History of Building and Loan in the United States.*

Table 2.1
Number of Associations, Shareholders, and Net Assets of Savings
and Loan Associations in the United States in 1893

State	Number of Associations	Number of Shareholders	Net Assets
Arkansas	69	19,493	$ 5,851,205
California	139	31,677	13,090,802
Colorado	60	16,950	5,088,004
Connecticut	15	3,222	433,578
Delaware	24	5,331	2,410,862
Dist. of Columbia	32	24,451	6,821,861
Georgia	37	10,453	3,137,603
Florida	37	10,524	3,159,418
Illinois	518	146,571	55,821,888
Indiana	350	90,157	21,390,550
Iowa	100	36,865	9,049,310
Kansas	164	46,330	13,907,211
Louisiana	21	6,569	3,391,557
Maine	36	10,064	2,020,293
Maryland	100	62,294	14,921,607
Massachusetts	115	54,484	14,574,334
Michigan	99	27,968	8,395,207
Minnesota	91	25,708	7,716,806
Mississippi	41	11,393	3,726,291
Missouri	418	74,620	35,446,429
Nebraska	47	13,278	3,985,603
New Hampshire	17	8,857	1,137,719
New Jersey	282	87,019	30,871,644
New York	447	156,660	32,820,563
Ohio	723	227,535	59,204,826
Pennsylvania	1,100	254,918	80,860,976
Rhode Island	7	2,506	791,410
Tennessee	143	40,398	12,126,410
Utah	11	3,108	932,801
Wisconsin	67	18,928	5,681,605
All Other States (estimated)	450	127,125	38,160,032
Total	5,860	1,655,456	496,928,405

Source: Financial Review and American Building Association News, 13:10, January
1894.

Table 2.2
The Growth of Savings and Loan Activity in the United States from 1893 to 1950

Date	No. of Assoc. in Thousands	Assets in Billions of Dollars	Date	No. of Assoc. in Thousands	Assets in Billions of Dollars
1893	5.8	.5	1923	10.7	3.9
1894	5.9	.60	1924	11.8	4.8
1895	6.0	.62	1925	12.4	5.5
1896	6.0	.65	1926	12.6	6.3
1897	5.9	.67	1927	12.8	7.2
1898	5.6	.66	1928	12.6	8.0
1899	5.6	.62	1929	12.3	8.7
1900	5.5	.60	1930	11.8	8.8
1901	5.4	.60	1931	11.4	8.4
1902	5.4	.61	1932	10.9	7.7
1903	5.3	.60	1933	10.7	7.0
1904	5.3	.62	1934	10.9	6.4
1905	5.3	.65	1935	10.5	5.9
1906	5.4	.69	1936	10.2	5.6
1907	5.5	.75	1937	9.7	5.7
1908	5.6	.80	1938	8.9	5.6
1909	5.7	.86	1939	8.3	5.7
1910	5.9	.95	1940	7.1	5.7
1911	6.1	1.0	1941	6.9	6.0
1912	6.3	1.1	1942	6.5	6.1
1913	6.4	1.2	1943	6.4	6.6
1914	6.6	1.4	1944	6.3	7.5
1915	6.8	1.5	1945	6.1	8.7
1916	7.0	1.6	1946	6.1	10.2
1917	7.3	1.8	1947	6.0	11.7
1918	7.5	1.9	1948	6.0	13.0
1919	7.8	2.1	1949	6.0	14.7
1920	8.6	2.5	1950	6.0	16.8
1921	9.3	2.9			
1922	10.0	3.3			

Sources: *Saving and Home Finance Source Book, 1954* (Washington, D.C.: Home Loan Bank Board), p. 6; U.S. Bureau of the Census, *Historical Statistics of the United States, 1789–1945* (Washington, D.C., 1949) p. 175; and H. Morton Bodfish,(ed.), *History of Building and Loan in the United States* (Chicago: United States Building and Loan League, 1931), p. 136.

tate company. However, its organizational structure was characteristic of the nation's early S & Ls.

It was not until the 1880s that modern-style thrifts appeared in Texas. In 1880 the state's first new-order S & L was organized, called the Dallas Homestead and Loan Association. This institution, which had no terminating feature (as we saw with the Oxford Provident), remained in operation until 1938, at which time it was liquidated and dissolved.[23] However, the Dallas-based association was, during these years, unique; the great majority of turn-of-the-century S & L charters were of the terminating variety. Thus a more comprehensive understanding of early S & L history requires an examination of charter plans—those provided by most pioneer thrift institutions.

THE MODERN S & L PLAN

As the U.S. savings and loan industry has grown in size (as measured in number of associations and in assets), it has evolved from a temporary undertaking to one characterized by permanence. This growth, and consequent permanence, resulted from the implementation of various S & L plans. The following chronicles the development of these plans.

Strictly speaking, an S & L plan is simply an agreement between an individual association and its members, one that governs both the life of the association and the manner in which shares[24] are to be issued and earnings distributed. Throughout U.S. S & L history four basic plans have bound together associations and their members: the terminating plan, the serial plan, the permanent plan, and the permanent stock plan.[25]

The plan exercised by founders of the Oxford Provident was of the "terminating" variety. Under this scheme, parties agreed to a simple, orderly process of saving for the purpose of buying or building homes. The plan stipulated that members simultaneously subscribe to the organization's stock and share, on a pro rata basis, accumulated funds. It further required that, in order for an individual to join an established plan, he contribute an amount sufficient to match the holdings of established members.

In most cases the terminating plan was most successful, particularly when all members were required to borrow from the association. In such cases the individual selected to receive the loan was chosen either through a lottery or in open bidding. It is important to note that these original terminating-plan institutions were not organized with profit per se in mind; instead, each represented a cooperative venture with a clear humanitarian objective: securing home ownership for individuals and families.[26] Indeed, these associations continued until, in each case, members' loans were secured.

The serial plan differed from the terminating plan in that while the latter made only one stock issue (to mature at a set time, usually within ten years), the former provided for periodic stock issues—which made it easier for members to join once operations had begun.[27] By continuing to offer further series of stocks, serial-plan associations achieved some measure of permanence; however, as with terminating-plan institutions, stock would mature on a set date, and ownership in the association was terminated accordingly.

Another difference between the two plans was that while the terminating plan granted each share of stock a pro rata sharing in the association's total funds, the serial plan afforded shareholders the same form of ownership with *each series* of stock issues. In effect, a serial plan association offered a group of terminating plans, with an overarching, yet segregated, collection of funds. Not surprisingly, then, the volume of funds in a typical serial-plan institution exceeded that of its terminating-plan counterpart. The higher volume was also accounted for by the fact that serial-plan entities dropped the requirement that members must borrow, thereby increasing their membership potential.

The next step in the evolution of U.S. S & Ls came in the form of the permanent-plan association. While this type offered an operation patterned primarily after the serial plan, it offered refinements and, in the minds of its owners, improvements. Basically, it provided for the sale of stock on demand, thereby eliminating the necessity of waiting (until a formal date of issue was set) or having to match the funds, on a pro rata basis, of existing members. Instead, the permanent S & L plan allowed investors the advantage of opening accounts in virtually the same, simple manner as they could with full-service banks.

A major innovation offered with the permanent plan involved this redemption of stock. While associations with serial and terminating plans required large, periodic redemption, and further required redemption of *all* stock at maturity, permanent-plan associations featured a more-or-less gradual, steady redemption of stock, owing to the unlimited number of issue dates.

The final S & L plan to emerge was the permanent-stock or guaranteed-stock plan. This scheme moved the S & L industry a step closer to corporate status, and one step further from the "mutual" ideal. The plan provided that, at the time of the association's establishment, a certain amount of stock, not redeemable, would be sold to investors. The investors would then have the opportunity to resell the stock. The permanent stock, because it would not be returned to stockholders, would act as a buffer against loss by new investors.

In addition to the nonwithdrawable feature, the permanent-stock plan provided a unique dividend scheme, which provided that no established (i.e., set) dividend apply to permanent stocks. Therefore, such stocks need not be subject to dividend rates comparable to that of ordinary stock.

Thus the appeal of the permanent-stock plan was twofold: for ordinary stockholders it provided a well-protected liquid investment; for the association's original investors, as for its organizers, it offered a very high-yield investment.

Of the four basic S & L plans that emerged in the industry's early history, the permanent and permanent-stock plans, as we have seen, offered the most promise both to original investors and to potential stockholders. As a result, today's S & L industry consists basically of these types of associations.

SUPERVISION AND CONGRESSIONAL CONCERN

Initially, legislation affecting S & Ls was enacted solely at the state level of government. New York was the first state to address this issue of S & L activity, by passing specific regulatory measures. In 1875 the state for the first time required "reports of condition" to be issued annually by all S & Ls. In 1892, New York went even further, then authorizing the compulsory supervision and annual inspection of all S & Ls by the state superintendent of banks.

Following the lead of the nation's largest state, more than half of the states had, by 1900, passed one or more laws regulating S & L operations. By 1931 all but two states had provided for some degree of regulation.[28]

Federal interest in the industry's activities increased during the 1890s and in 1894 Congress passed the Wilson Tariff Act, originally proposed as a law that would levy a tax on the net income of corporations. In its final (approved) version, the act contained a critical, precedent-setting provision: "Nothing herein contained shall apply to building and loan associations or companies which make loans only to their shareholders."[29] Thus Congress formally recognized, and moved to foster, the special function of S & Ls within the U.S. financial community. Moreover, it extended this exception in a dozen follow-up acts, involving tariffs or simple revenues, between the years 1897 and 1928.[30]

Another congressional move, passage of the Federal Reserve Act in 1913, has had a profound impact on the S & L industry. In addition to establishing a central banking system, this act provided a clear legal distinction between deposit types. Moreover, it set lower reserve requirements for time deposits, which could be withdrawn only with prior notice.

In the same year that Congress established the "Fed," Texas' S & Ls also underwent substantial changes. Prior to 1913 each of these associations had obtained a charter through a special act of the state legislature. But that year the thirty-third legislature passed House Bill 17, the state's first general law pertaining to S & Ls. Under HB 17 the state provided for the incorporation and regulation of building and loan associations, the supervision and control of which would come from the Commissioner of Insurance and Banking.[31]

Throughout this era of new supervision and control, the S & L industry grew at a rapid, steady rate. Total assets of S & Ls, only $.5 billion in 1893, amounted to $2.5 billion by 1920.[32] During the "Roaring Twenties," growth was even more as-

tounding: between 1920 and 1930 industry assets increased by
$6.3 billion, to total $8.8 billion.[33] So, as the nation approached
its most severe economic depression, S & Ls were in excellent
financial shape.

ENDURING THE GREAT DEPRESSION

By the end of 1930 U.S. S & Ls were realizing the impact of
the Great Depression. Symptomatic of this was the dramatically increasing rate of withdrawals of funds from S & Ls, a
practice that would peak in the years 1933–34.[34] Furthermore,
despite the relatively long-term loans offered by S & Ls, the
rate of timely loan repayments began to decline markedly; in
many cases, this led to foreclosure.

The depression-related problems facing S & Ls were not iso-
lated; at the same time, bank failures were mounting at an
alarming rate. In fact, between 1930 and 1933 more than 8,800
commercial banks failed, a development that indirectly hurt
S & Ls, as thousands of their customers lost bank deposits.[35]

A common depression-era problem for all financial institutions was home foreclosure, especially in urban areas. Prior to
the depression, urban foreclosures totaled about 75,000 annually, but in 1933 alone 271,000 families lost homes to foreclosures.[36] Consequently, S & Ls, with thousands of new property holdings, found themselves immersed in the real estate
business. Still, notwithstanding the sharp decline in real estate
values during the depression years, thrift institutions suffered
relatively mild losses. In most cases associations held and
maintained their properties, realized fair rental incomes from
them, and, following the depression, sold most of them at or
near their initial costs.[37]

Yet despite the modest impact of home foreclosures, the
overall effect of the depression on S & Ls was considerable. Besides halting the industry's predepression growth, the economic downturn resulted in a loss of assets in excess of $3 bil-
lion. Moreover, nearly one-half of all S & Ls fell victim to
financial problems: in 1925 the United States boasted more than
12,000 thrifts; by 1941 the number was less than 7,000.[38]

By the decade of the 1930s the federal government, which

already had begun shaping S & L activities nationwide, faced a major challenge: How could the nation's savings and loan industry be saved? Its response was immediate and ambitious. First, in 1932, Congress created the Federal Home Loan Bank System (FHLBS). This was followed a year later by the establishment of the Home Owners Loan Corporation (HOLC) which, until 1936, itself provided home loans. Indeed, during its three active years the HOLC refinanced about $.75 billion worth of home mortgages, on more than 1 million homes formerly financed privately.[39] Furthermore, when taxes, assessments, closing costs, and reconditioning loans are included in the total, the HOLC advanced nearly $3.1 billion.[40]

During these early depression years Congress also created the Federal Deposit Insurance Corporation (FDIC) in 1933, and passed the Federal Savings and Loan Insurance Corporation (FSLIC) Act in 1934. With the FDIC Congress effectively insured deposits in commercial banks, while the FSLIC provided similar protection for S & L savings accounts.[41]

Another important component of federal involvement in affairs of the financial community was government's direct financial investment—nearly $275 million, deposited among some 1,400 S & Ls nationwide. This government investment involved two vehicles: First, the U.S. Treasury invested $49.3 million in federal associations. Second, the HOLC was authorized to invest up to $300 million in both federal and state-chartered associations. These funds were targeted, in the main, at the creation of new institutions.[42]

In Texas, the depression years reflected the national economic climate. Between 1930 and 1936 the state experienced pessimism, as well as economic contraction. During these years the number of state-chartered S & Ls fell from 176 to 87, with 16 others in liquidation.[43] At the same time, assets declined tremendously, from $137 million to about $60 million.[44]

Table 2.3 reflects the drop in number of state associations, and their dwindling resources, between the years 1929 and 1936. Of particular significance is the reduction in assets of all active state associations, totaling more than 50 percent.

By the late 1930s U.S. S & Ls, blessed with a vastly improved real estate market throughout most of the nation, enjoyed re-

Table 2.3
Number and Assets of Texas Savings and Loan Associations, 1929–36

Year	Number of Associations	Total Assets
1929	176 state	$137,015,903
1930	155 state	134,743,150
1931	145 state	127,285,977
1932	144 state	114,631,152
1933	139 active state	100,393,588
	4 liquidating state	742,712
	143 total	101,136,300
1934	130 active state	82,886,876
	3 liquidating state	479,561
	54 federal	3,556,150
	187 total	86,922,587
1935	98 active state	61,742,963
	14 liquidating state	1,960,873
	86 federal	14,366,932
	198 total	70,070,768
1936	95 active state	59,246,444
	14 liquidating state	1,716,330
	88 federal	18,468,693
	197 total	79,427,467

Sources: *Annual Report of Building and Loan Associations, 1929–1936; Building and Loan Annals,* 1930–37.

newed prosperity. As the United States sat on the verge of entry into World War II, the industry's real estate holdings had been substantially reduced. In addition, as lending for construction regained viability, total loan volume increased considerably. Finally, because the depression had prompted the modernization of many S & Ls' operations, industry officials emerged from this period of general bleakness with changed attitudes about practices concerning liquidity, reserves, interest and dividend rates, lending and savings plans, advertising, and the proper role of managers and directors. As we shall see shortly, a series of sweeping changes would soon reflect these changed attitudes.[45]

THE DUAL SYSTEM OF CHARTERS

The charter under which an association operates is a contract between the governing body and the association. An S & L may be chartered by the national government or by the state in which it intends to operate. The actual charter may be long or short, detailed or general, depending upon the statutes under which it exists. Prior to 1933 only states granted association charters, but in that year the Home Owners Loan Act provided for the incorporation of federal S & Ls, under the administration of the Federal Home Loan Bank Board.[46]

A typical state charter is brief and simple. It includes, in most cases, little more than the name of the association, its purpose, its place of business, the names and residences of its members, the initial amount of savings capital held by each member, the duration of the charter, and the number, names, and residences of directors, along with their respective tenures of office.[47]

The objective of the national government in creating federal charters for some S & Ls was to promote stability and uniformity among savings associations nationwide. Thus the formal authorization for these came in 1933, with the signing into law of the Home Owners Loan Act. Despite the generally held view that the new federal charters and their accompanying regulations represented an improvement over existing state charters, many problems plagued early federal S & Ls. As a result, rules changes, enacted in 1936 and 1949, were needed to simplify the original regulations and charters, so as to provide S & Ls greater flexibility in their operations.[48]

An association may be governed by one or more of four general systems of regulatory control or influence: the Federal Savings and Loan System; the Federal Savings and Loan Insurance System; the Federal Home Loan Bank System; and the various state regulatory systems. Because of various demands made by certain of these regulatory agencies, an association may decide to change charters (i.e., from state charter to federal charter, or vice versa). During the 1930s, as the federal government laid its heavy hand on virtually every aspect of finance and economics nationwide, the nation witnessed a substantial increase in the number and percentage of federal charters. However, since World War II this trend has been reversed, and state charters have emerged as most popular.

For those who favor a strict system of checks and balances, the dual system of charters offers a distinct advantage over the uniform system of state charters. That is, with dual charters there exists an ongoing competition between federal regulatory agencies and the various state agencies. Consequently, individual institutions enjoy, on occasion, the luxury of conflict between the agencies, as it oftentimes leads to desirable innovations. Moreover, while such innovations may be expected in the absence of the dual system, they probably occur more rapidly under this system.[49]

WORLD WAR II AND ITS AFTERMATH

More than ever before, World War II swept the S & L industry into the larger business community. To a very great extent this was a function of the national government's wartime resolve to link government and business. At the same time, S & L executives representing even small communities came to depend heavily on war bond drives. Indeed, many such executives assumed posts of responsibility with draft boards, rationing boards, "fair rent" committees, and, in some larger cities, even civil defense programs.[50] Throughout the nation, then, S & Ls, like other businesses, became increasingly tied to government.

Following the bombing of Pearl Harbor on December 7, 1941, shortages of building materials and priority systems[51] resulted in a dramatic slowdown in private homebuilding nationwide. This prompted many S & L officials to engage in government programs, as an alternative. Also, because of the reduction in building competition, construction loans on existing properties took on special significance. Yet, on the other hand, savings opportunities were enhanced as a direct result of wartime economics, and many associations had an abundance of funds. So the aim of the national government, to sell its bonds to institutional investors, was consistent with the associations' desire

Table 2.4

Government Securities Owned by Savings and Loan Associations and Ratio to Total Assets, 1938–46 (in millions of dollars)

Year	U.S. Government Securities	Total Assets	Ratio
1938	$ 75	$ 5,632	1.3%
1939	73	5,597	1.3
1940	71	5,733	1.2
1941	107	6,049	1.8
1942	318	6,150	5.2
1943	853	6,604	12.9
1944	1,671	7,458	22.4
1945	2,420	8,747	27.7
1946	2,009	10,202	19.7

Source: Federal Home Loan Bank Board, *Savings and Home Financing Source Book*, 1961, p. 8.

for new investment outlets.[52] All in all, the wartime economy was far from damaging to the nation's S & L industry.

Table 2.4 reveals the impact of S & L bond purchases on their balance sheets. In 1940, government securities amounted to only 1.2 percent of total S & L assets; by 1945 they represented nearly 28 percent of assets. This trend was particularly pronounced in Texas: in 1941, approximately $.5 million in U.S. government bonds were held by Texas institutions; by 1945 the amount had swelled to over $16 million.[53]

Clearly, one outstanding feature of the immediate post–World War II era was expansion by the S & L industry. From coast to coast associations did what they could to meet the challenge of the great housing shortage and the corresponding demand for mortgage funds. Because they emerged from the war with ample liquid resources (over $2 billion), U.S. S & Ls were able to undertake large-scale financing of home mortgages.[54] Beyond home mortgaging, the S & L industry had, by the late 1940s, developed a broad sense of mission. Across the nation, institutions placed renewed emphasis on attractive quarters, choice locations, and business-promotion activities.

The postwar mission of U.S. S & Ls was shaped largely by the federal government, which, in 1950, enacted critically important statutory changes affecting the S & L industry. Hence that year represented the beginning of the modern S & L era. It is to the early years of this era that we now turn.

NOTES

1. U.S. Constitution art. I, sec. 4. This section deals with the "taxation" powers given Congress and reads: "The Congress shall have power . . . to make all laws which shall be necessary and proper for carrying into execution the foregoing powers, and all other powers vested by this constitution in the Government of the United States, or in any department or offices thereof."

2. U.S. Constitution, art. I, sec. 8. Under this clause, Congress is empowered to regulate commerce with other nations as well as between the states.

3. The power of the states to enact such legislation is less obvious, at least to members of the Supreme Court. Indeed, such power is found, albeit without specific reference, in the Constitution's Tenth Amendment. Therein, the states are granted all powers that are not reserved for the national government. If indeed it were to be held that all such bank-related powers are reserved for the national government, then perhaps the Ninth Amendment, which allows for a sharing of powers, could be construed to permit the states to pass such legislation. In any case, the states do, under guidelines established by Congress, regulate state-chartered banks and other financial institutions.

4. John Donovan (ed.), *Democracy at the Crossroads* (New York: Holt, Rinehart and Winston, 1978), p. 373. Significantly, this decision could conceivably result in a future court radically reinterpreting the "commerce" or "necessary and proper" clause, or the constitutionality of any number of other laws.

5. Ronàld E. Pynn, *American Politics: Changing Expectations* (Monterey, Calif.: Brooks/Cole, 1984) p. 107. Often overlooked in this decision is the Court's insistence that neither level of government may tax the other. This reasoning was simple: the power to tax, the Court said, is the power to destroy, and neither the national government nor the states shall be empowered to destroy the other.

6. Sidney Ratner, James Soltow, Richard Sylla, *The Evolution of the American Economy* (New York: Basic Books, 1979), p. 158.

7. *Ibid.*, p. 363.

8. The original "savings and loan associations" were called "building and loan associations." Not until the last few decades did the name "savings and loan" become commonplace.

9. Jack Cashin,"History of Savings and Loan Associations in Texas," Doctoral Dissertation, University of Texas, 1955, p. 6.

10. H. Morton Bodfish (ed.), *History of Building and Loan in the United States* (Chicago: United States Building and Loan League, 1931), pp. 32–34.

11. The name "Oxford Provident" was given to the first savings and loan in the United States. Oxford was the previous name of the town Frankford and the word Provident had the connotation of being thrifty.

12. Bodfish, pp. 37–42.

13. Alan Teck, *Mutual Savings Banks and Savings and Loan Associations: Aspects of Growth* (New York: Columbia University Press, 1968), p. 23.

14. *Ibid.*

15. Bodfish, p. 40.

16. *Ibid.*

17. Teck, p. 24.

18. Bodfish, pp. 70–71.

19. Teck, p. 24.

20. Bodfish, p. 68.

21. Cashin, p. 39.

22. *Ibid.*, p. 41.

23. *Ibid.*, p. 42.

24. A "share" represented ownership in a particular S & L. For example, in the Oxford Provident Association a "share" sold for $500.00. Members were allowed to make an initial payment and contribute on a monthly basis until the share was fully purchased.

25. Horace F. Clark and Frank A. Chase, *Elements of the Modern Building and Loan Associations* (New York: Macmillan, 1925), p. 33.

26. That is, though in most cases profits necessarily accrue to home owners, the objective was home ownership, not money making.

27. Cashin, p. 30.

28. Leon T. Kendall, *The Savings and Loan Business* (Englewood Cliffs, N.J.: Prentice-Hall, 1962), p. 6.

29. Josephine Ewalt, *A Business Reborn: The Savings and Loan Story, 1930–1960* (Chicago: American Savings and Loan Institute Press, 1962), p. 390.

30. *Ibid.* The most important of these were the 1897 Dingley Tariff Act, the 1898 War Revenue Act, and the 1909 Payne-Aldrich Tariff Act.

31. Cashin, p. 51.

32. Ewalt, p. 391.

33. *Ibid.*
34. Kendall, p. 6.
35. *Ibid.*
36. Kendall, p. 7.
37. *Ibid.*
38. *Ibid.*
39. *Ibid.*
40. *Ibid.*
41. Robert Hoover, "The Behavioral Responses of Thrift Institutions to the Garn-St. Germain Depository Institutions Act of 1982," Master's Thesis, University of Texas, 1985, p. 12.
42. Kendall, p. 7.
43. Cashin, p. 113.
44. Part of this decrease resulted from conversion of funds from state to federal savings and loans, a common practice during the depression.
45. Kendall, p. 8.
46. Kendall, p. 22.
47. *Ibid.*
48. *Ibid.*, p. 23.
49. *Ibid.*, p. 29.
50. Ewalt, p. 201.
51. A "priority system" was set up during World War II where restrictions on the use of materials, especially metals, were set by the federal government. Homebuilding, not being a war-related industry, was limited during the first half of the 1940s.
52. Ewalt, p. 202.
53. Cashin, pp. 148–56. One other change in the quality of Texas S & L assets deserves mention. In 1937 state S & Ls owned in excess of $10 million worth of real estate other than office buildings. By 1945 this figure was reduced to slightly over $1 million. The years of World War II were indeed marked by S & L liquidation of real estate assets, and Texas-based S & Ls were simply a part of the liquidation movement.
54. Kendall, p. 8.

3

Problems in the Postwar Years: National and Texas State S & Ls, 1950–65

Between the years 1950 and 1965 the S & L industry in the United States experienced considerable change, for a variety of reasons. These changes resulted from the industry's rapid growth and various problems that attended that growth. In this chapter we explore the costs and unintended consequences of S & L blossoming in the United States, and particularly within Texas, during these years of national economic expansion.

Of special significance to Texas are the two distinctly different phases of S & L development during this era. During the decade of the 1950s, Texas S & Ls, like the majority of U.S. thrifts, were lulled into a false sense of security, based on their huge year-to-year deposit growth rates and fairly stable interest rates. But in the 1960s Texas S & L leaders, sensing potential trouble, demanded change, including freedom from control by the state's banking commissioner and an overhaul of the state S & L code.

In making these demands during a time of general economic prosperity Texas' S & Ls displayed boldness but considerable foresight as well. Indeed, within a few years after implementation of these changes other states' industry members began pressuring their respective political leaders for operational changes similar to those enacted in Texas. Thus the Lone Star State, in characteristically independent fashion, has pioneered, through its state-chartered S & Ls, a wave of innovation that eventually would rock the nation's entire financial community.

INDUSTRY PROBLEMS

The difficulties encountered by U.S. S & Ls in the 1950s are somewhat characteristic of those troubling modern S & Ls, particularly those in Texas. It is therefore beneficial to view this period with more than an eye for historical trivia, if we are determined to avoid duplicating our past mistakes. Moreover, the lessons learned from U.S. S & L history have a value that transcends the narrow world of finance, as they stem from a common dilemma: how to cope with newly realized prosperity.

A long-standing problem facing S & Ls nationwide, one that continues to threaten the industry's prospects for recovery, is that of simple interest risk. That is, whenever an association borrows, lends, or establishes an interest rate, it incurs some measure of risk. The degree of risk depends upon external factors (e.g., the nation's money supply, the housing market, construction costs, inflation, etc.) as well as the peculiar characteristics of a given S & L (e.g., its management, level of reserves, outstanding accounts, etc.). Hence, well-managed institutions, unlikely to face severe internal problems, generally respond better to large-scale crises than do their fiscally inferior competitors.

All financial institutions keep a close eye on the single most important barometer of the market—the interest rate. However fiscally sound an S & L may be, it cannot afford to ignore signals that rates are nearing fluctuation. For healthy S & Ls, such a mistake can lead to heavy dollar losses; for weaker associations it can—and often does—result in insolvency.

During times of relative calm and prosperity it matters little if an institution pays minimal heed to interest rates. However, when economic conditions worsen, it is the institution's adjustment to these rates that, in most instances, will determine its fate. This is because most S & Ls have "mismatched" maturities. Stated simply, this means that they have borrowed through the use of short-term instruments (mainly savings accounts), but lent via long-term assets (mainly housing mortgages). Such mismatching becomes a serious problem whenever inflation causes large increases in the cost of funds available to S & Ls, without corresponding increases in long-term mortgage payments, which typically were fixed at relatively low interest rates during times of low inflation. If over a period of time the cost of funds continues to exceed income earned from assets, insolvency is inevitable.[1]

Another chronic S & L problem involves the nondiversification of portfolios. That is, whenever an institution concentrates too heavily on mortgage lending, it faces, especially during times of housing-market depression, grave problems.[2] Unfortunately for U.S. S & Ls, government regulations, coupled with tax laws, made it difficult during the 1950s for them to limit risk through portfolio diversification.[3] Thus it was good fortune, not clever portfolio strategies, that throughout this decade of strong housing enabled institutions to avoid problems resulting from nondiversification. Nevertheless, the potential for disaster was apparent by the early 1950s.

A third industry concern, one that is ongoing, involves liquidity. As a problem inherent to lending institutions, it threatens institutional stability whenever the great preponderance of an S & L's assets are committed to long-term, fixed-rate mortgage loans. In fairness to the nation's S & Ls, there was not, until very recently, more than a limited secondary market for assets, so their reliance on these mortgages was unavoidable. (Today, many government-sponsored programs[4] provide a secondary market for the sale of mortgage loans; without them, today's S & Ls, with few exceptions, would be facing greater liquidity problems).[5]

Other opportunities unseized by S & Ls until very recently include construction loans and larger consumer loans. With construction loans (or outright construction investment) in particular, S & Ls operating in the 1950s could have secured profits from a wide assortment of fast-growing, profitable commercial property investment ventures. (As it was, Texas state-chartered S & Ls were the first in the United States to become involved in such projects; later, following passage of the Depository Institution's Deregulation and Monetary Control Act in 1980, and the Garn-St. Germain Depository Institutions Act of 1982—both of which are explored at length in Chapter 5—federally chartered S & Ls began to engage in such ventures.)

The significance of the development of these new investment opportunities cannot be overstated. It means that, unlike institutions of the 1950s and 1960s, today's S & Ls, though plagued by the same uncertain economic conditions as their predecessors, have the freedom to shift, when necessary, from heavy emphasis on long-term mortgage loans to greater reliance on short-term construction and consumer loans. This increases their diversity and liquidity, and can work to "buy" time for institutions facing hard times. Had such options been available to 1950s S & Ls, many problems that occurred during the three succeeding decades might well have been avoided.

Another difficulty confronting S & Ls is that of geographic limitation, which stems from both federal and state laws and regulations. Extremely rigid "lending limits," usually 50 or 100 miles from the main office of an institution, have negated many thousands of potential loans. An important residual effect of such limitations is higher interest rates, the direct result of restricted competition.[6]

All told, these problems account for the crisis that, in recent years, culminated in the revamping of the S & L industry. In order to objectively understand the problems facing today's institutions, then, it is necessary to be mindful of the circumstances under which their long-standing difficulties originated.

GROWTH IN THE S & L INDUSTRY: 1950–65

Despite the aforementioned potential hindrances to S & L prosperity during the decade of the 1950s, these nonetheless were years of unprecedented industry growth. Indeed, measured in dollar value such growth, in Texas and nationwide, surpassed the expectations of even the most optimistic industry analysts. Nationally, assets of S & Ls in 1950 totaled $16.9

billion; ten years later assets had swelled to $71.5 billion. Within Texas the growth was even more impressive. During the same ten-year period state S & L assets jumped from $390 million to $2.5 billion—a sixfold increase.[7]

Many factors spawned S & L growth during this decade of generally good economic times. Among the most important of these was the accelerated growth in housing mortgages, which constituted the industry's backbone. In fact, such mortgage growth led, during the same period, to growth of GNP, disposable personal income, and population.[8] Contributing in large part to the rosy housing market was passage of the 1949 Housing Act, which established a national housing goal of "a decent home and suitable living environment for every American family."[9] Specifically, the act provided grants to municipalities for public housing and slum clearance, along with a program of financial assistance for rural areas (under the Farmers Home Administration).[10] Spurred by the government-set goal of housing for all, along with a series of rules and tax laws designed to assist those S & Ls specializing—as reflected in their portfolios—in mortgage loans, the housing market was destined to expand greatly, as it did.[11]

A second important factor contributing to industry improvement was the preferential tax treatment given S & Ls—but not to other financial institutions—as a result of long-standing government policy. Such favoritism began with the Wilson Tariff Act of 1894, which provided S & Ls a tax exemption.[12] Under this act, all other corporations were subject to a 2 percent tax on net income, but the law stated that "nothing herein contained shall apply to building and loan associations or companies which make loans only to their shareholders."[13]

In 1951, however, the Revenue Act of that year removed S & Ls from the list of tax-exempt corporations, forcing them to pay taxes at the rate paid by commercial banks. The law, which took effect on September 1, 1951, specifically removed all S & Ls from the exemption, regardless of whether they operated for profit, and irrespective of their charter types.[14] Although the Revenue Act removed S & Ls from the category of tax-exempt corporations, it did permit them to build free reserves, to the level of 12 percent of withdrawable shares.

Because of this action a great tax advantage was enjoyed by all U.S. S & Ls, as it allowed for considerable business expense—and consequently a generous deduction on gross income. Indeed, owing to this provision only one Texas S & L, between the years 1951 and 1963, paid *any* corporate income tax.[15] Until 1963, when tax laws were altered once more, this freedom from virtually any tax threat provided thrifts a critical edge in their competition with commercial banks and was instrumental in their overall prosperity during the decade of the 1950s.

While the 1949 Housing Act and the 1951 Revenue Act were the most significant regulatory changes to foster rapid S & L growth during the 1950s and early 1960s, other changes contributed to this expansion as well. One of these, in 1952, was an amendment to the federal government's Defense Production Act. This legislation gave S & Ls flexibility in lending by easing down payment requirements on a gradual basis. Consequently, institutions were able to provide mortgages to individuals with only modest savings.[16]

Another boost for S & Ls came in 1953, when housing amendments vastly improved the housing market by making mortgages more attractive to institutions and more accessible to potential buyers. Among other things, this legislation repealed a provision that prohibited the absorption of Veterans Administration (VA) discounts; this meant a return to the practice of providing discounts on VA loans in spite of interest-rate floors otherwise requiring S & Ls to charge higher rates.

The law opened further avenues of mortgage expansion via the Federal National Mortgage Association (FNMA) by providing: (1) the transfer of a portion of $900 million, earmarked for military, defense, and disaster mortgages, to a fund for the purchase of Federal Housing Administration (FHA) and VA mortgages; and (2) a so-called one-for-one program, wherein the FNMA could strike a deal with a lender holding an FNMA mortgage in which the FNMA would, within one year, purchase an equal amount from the given lender. So popular was the latter provision that the $500 million authorization for the program was exhausted in less than one year, as it proved particularly attractive to builders in search of short-term, interim financing for construction projects.[17]

In the following year the Housing Act (1954) altered several statutes governing S & Ls. Specifically, the law raised the maximum an S & L could lend from $20,000 to $35,000; and Federal Home Loan Banks were authorized to accept as collateral mortgages with maturities as lengthy as 25 years (previously, the limit was 20 years).[18]

In the latter half of the decade national laws governing S & Ls continued to reflect the liberalization of federal S & L policy. First, in 1956, the FHA reduced down payment requirements on low-priced houses ($9,000 or less). That same year saw the FHLBB increase the percentage of savings capital that institutions could use for credit lines. Finally, during this same year the FNMA lowered the stock-purchase requirement on the value of mortgages sold.[19]

Two years later Congress, responding to a modest national recession, passed the Emergency Housing law. This act provided an interest-rate ceiling on VA loans of only 4.75 percent. In addition, FHA mortgage regulations were liberalized: the agency was allowed to issue mortgage loans when borrowers were able to put up as little as 3 percent of the houses' values, up to the first $13,500 of each house.[20]

Congress went even further in 1959, lowering once again the minimum down payment schedule for FHA loans. Moreover, the national legislature provided S & Ls higher mortgage limits on FHA-insured one- and two-family units. Finally, Congress gave thrifts limited authority to make loans for financing the acquisition and development of land.[21]

While the early years of the 1960s brought few changes in laws and regulations governing S & L activity, a few critical changes did have a measurable impact on the industry. The first of these involved an amendment to the federal guidelines covering S & L taxation. Effective in 1963, the new law increased these institutions' federal tax liability, while establishing a complex series of rules regarding their tax status.[22]

In the following year, Congress passed the 1964 Housing Act, which incorporated the most crucial changes in S & L legislation of the post–World War II era—at least until that time. First, the law extended the lending area of all FSLIC-insured institutions from 50 miles to 100 miles, thereby increasing the competition for loans among clustered S & Ls. The act further empowered federal associations to invest in obligations issued by states, political subdivisions,[23] and federal agencies.

A unique section of the 1964 law gave S & Ls authority to issue unsecured personal loans for the payment of expenses related to college education. This provision represented a radical departure from previous guidelines, as it also stood as one of the few times Congress granted financial institutions the right to make loans not directly related to real estate financing.

Two final changes shaped S & L practices in the first five years of the 1960s. In 1964 the FHLBB introduced a new reserve regulation that affected the growth, and portfolio status, of most insured S & Ls. Specifically the regulation improved the quality of loan portfolios but somewhat reduced borrowing opportunities of some potential homeowners.[24] Finally, in 1965, the FHLBB established more stringent policies governing the conditions under which advances could be obtained from regional Home Loan Banks.

In retrospect, it seems that the most important stimulant to national S & L growth during the 1950s, irrespective of legal changes, was the absence of competition from commercial banks. Indeed, as seen in Table 3.1, average annual yields between 1950 and 1960 were, without exception, higher for S & Ls than for commerical banks. In fact, throughout the early 1950s S & Ls were paying, on the average, more than twice the interest paid by commercial banks. For the entire decade S & L yields were, on the average, 150 basis points above commercial bank yields.[25]

The fact is, commercial banks were not, in the early postwar years, terribly concerned about savings deposits. This was evidenced by banks' yield-structure policies during this era. Then, a common practice of theirs was to pay a certain interest rate on savings deposits, up to a specified limit (e.g., 2 percent on deposits not exceeding $2,000); thereafter, deposits exceeding the established ceiling would draw a lower—often as much as 25 percent lower—rate of interest. This practice, needless to

Table 3.1
Average Annual Yield on Selected Types of Investments, 1950–60

Year	Sav. Acts. in Savings Associations	Sav. Deps. in Mutual Sav. Bks.	Time & Sav. Deps. in Coml. Bks.	United States Govt. Bnds.
1950	2.5%	1.9%	.9%	2.3%
1951	2.6	2.0	1.1	2.6
1952	2.7	2.3	1.1	2.7
1953	2.8	2.4	1.1	2.9
1954	2.9	2.5	1.3	2.5
1955	2.9	2.6	1.4	2.8
1956	3.0	2.8	1.6	3.1
1957	3.3	2.9	2.1	3.5
1958	3.38	3.07	2.21	3.43
1959	3.53	3.19	2.36	4.07
1960	3.86	3.47	2.56	4.01

Source: *U.S. Savings and Loan Fact Book, 1966.*

say, provided an enormous disincentive for potentially large depositors.

Beyond the disinterest in large deposits exhibited by many commercial banks, S & Ls had little other competition. To most depositors, thrifts seemed, for good reason, a preferable alternative to commercial banks, mutual savings banks, and even to U.S. savings bonds. This situation was ideal for S & Ls, most of which had an abundance of potential borrowers—those seeking home mortgage loans.

A final, very important factor contributing to S & L growth—in Texas and throughout the nation—during the 1950s was the good health of the U.S. economy. Indeed, by comparing population growth and GNP growth, we see that the explosion in housing—the single most important component of S & L success—during this era should have been expected. Between 1950 and 1960 the national population increased from 151 million to 180 million, while Texas' increase was 7.7 million to 9.6 million.[26] During this same period the gross national product (GNP) rose by an incredible 75 percent from $285 billion to $504 billion.[27]

Of equal importance was the increase in U.S. disposable in-

Table 3.2
Distribution of Total Personal Income, 1950–60 (dollar amounts in billions)

Year	Personal Income	Disposable Personal Income	Personal Savings Amount	Personal Savings As Pct. of Disposable Income
1950	$227.6	$206.9	$13.1	6.3%
1951	255.6	226.6	17.3	7.6
1952	272.5	238.3	18.1	7.6
1953	288.2	252.6	18.3	7.2
1954	290.1	257.4	16.4	6.4
1955	310.9	275.3	15.8	5.7
1956	333.0	293.2	20.6	7.0
1957	351.1	308.5	20.7	6.7
1958	361.2	318.8	22.3	7.0
1959	383.5	337.3	19.1	5.7
1960	401.0	350.0	17.0	4.9

Source: 1974 Savings and Loan Fact Book.

come over this same period: from $207 billion in 1950 to $350 billion in 1960. (In Texas the relative increase was just as impressive during these years, rising, on a per capita basis, from $1,339 to $1,924).[28] Another important statistic, particularly to financial institutions, is that of savings as a percentage of disposable income. Here, as revealed in Table 3.2, we see that, during the 1950s, Americans experienced substantial growth. The personal savings increase over the ten-year period averaged over 7 percent annually.

Other factors, less subject to easy measurement than the aforementioned, also contributed to S & L growth during the 1950s. For example, the general prosperity of the nation throughout the decade was accompanied by a permanently higher housing-price level and a conspicuous enlargement of the middle class—the segment of the population S & Ls rely on most for housing purchases.

This middle class of the 1950s sought a new life-style, one characterized in large part by suburban home ownership. This rush to the suburbs created mobility never before experienced in the United States, as these new suburbanites needed houses. S & Ls were eager to help finance these homes.

Table 3.3
Number of S & Ls in Texas, 1950–60

Year	State	Federal	Total
1950	62	83	145
1951	68	83	151
1952	77	82	159
1953	84	80	164
1954	89	80	169
1955	101	80	181
1956	111	81	192
1957	121	81	202
1958	134	81	215
1959	153	82	235
1960	159	83	242

Source: Texas Savings and Loan Department, "Annual Reports of Savings and Loan Associations."

Another important contributor to S & L growth in the 1950s was the confidence Americans displayed in the industry itself. This was due, to a great extent, to the popular recognition that thrifts were protected through the FSLIC's insurance program. With the backing of the world's richest government, how could depositors lose? Indeed, how could S & Ls lose?

FROM FEDERAL TO STATE CHARTERS

Along with the unprecedented growth of the U.S. national S & L industry in the 1950s came, in Texas, an important development in the state's thrift industry. As indicated in Table 3.3, state S & Ls began to outnumber those with federal charters as early as 1953. That is, while federal S & Ls numbered a majority in 1950, the next three years produced 22 new state-chartered S & Ls, but no new federally chartered institutions. In fact, during this time three federal thrifts switched to state charters. After 1953 the trend continued, so that by 1960 the number of Texas state-chartered institutions had, over ten years, increased by more than 150 percent, from 62 to 159, while the number of federal thrifts held steady at 83.

Many conditions within the S & L industry of the 1950s help to explain the dramatic increase in state charters. Much of the explanation could also serve to explain why institutions opted for federal charters, or converted to federal charters, prior to this time.

In the 1930s and 1940s many institutions preferred the status and prestige associated with the federal government, and so elected to apply for federal charters. Others, less conscious of image, did so simply to expedite insurance coverage, or to secure assistance that many analysts believed, would be most readily available to federal institutions. But once industry officials realized that federal charters brought neither prestige nor status nor superior financial assistance (nor, for that matter, an edge in obtaining insurance, as FSLIC insurance is available without preference to charter type), they reexamined their situations, and many converted to state charters, where, as we shall see, the real advantages lay.

Perhaps the most important advantage that state S & Ls were permitted was a stock form of ownership, whereas federal institutions were, until 1976, required to maintain a mutual form of ownership.[29] A permanent stock plan—available only to state-chartered institutions—is desirable for many reasons. Most importantly, there exists under such plans no requirement that permanent stockholders be paid dividends equal to those paid investors. Typically, organizers of S & Ls put great amounts of their own time, effort, and money into an association. While they may not expect immediate compensation if the venture succeeds, permanent stock is considered a form of reward for the additional risks they assumed.

Another reason for the rise in state-chartered S & Ls is that many industry officials believe that local regulation is, by virtue of its proximity if nothing else, better suited for most associations, particularly during times of local troubles. Though the existence of 12 district Home Loan Banks (the regulatory and supervisory agencies for federal S & Ls) somewhat offsets this argument, many businessmen, like most S & L leaders, continue to prefer state control. They believe, first, that local regulation is preferable to federal regulation (however physically close it may be), and, second, that their customers feel more comfortable with local control.

A final reason accounting for the popularity of state incorporation is that in some states, Texas included, state-chartered institutions are given greater latitude than their federal counterparts in the range of loans and investments available to them. For example, during the 1950s state institutions were permitted to engage in certain personal lending transactions, while federally chartered S & Ls nonmortgage activities were restricted, basically, to investment in government bonds.[30]

LAWS AFFECTING TEXAS S & Ls

On July 2, 1929, the forty-first Texas Legislature passed Senate Bill 111 that, in its original form, was to be the "Texas S & L Code" for the next 34 years.[31] Most significantly, the new code placed state S & Ls under the control of the Texas banking commissioner, thus unsurping the authority of the state Board of Insurance Commissioners. Not until 1963 was a complete revision of the Texas S & L code completed. Prior to that year the only changes in the 1929 code were minor, usually of a technical nature.

The four main areas of the 1929 Code were Section 1, which dealt with the definition of what characterizes a building and loan association; Section 7, which describes supervision and control of S & Ls; Section 26, which deals with restrictions on the types of loans S & Ls could make; and Section 36, which describes the nature of an S & L association.

These four sections of the early Texas S & L code were the cornerstones of the state's body of thrift regulatory legislation during the 1950s, at a time when these institutions, like those throughout the United States, were involved almost exclusively in the business of home mortgages. But this general function would change—as would the laws and regulations governing Texas' state-chartered institutions.

INDEPENDENCE FOR TEXAS S & Ls: 1961–65

In addition to the rapid growth in Texas' S & L activities between the years 1960 and 1965, the period was significant because of the creation of the position of Texas savings and loan commissioner in 1961 and the adoption of a new S & L code in 1963. Together, these developments allowed state-chartered S & Ls to become leaders in financial innovations within our nation's thrift industry.

So rapid was growth among Texas state-chartered S & Ls in the 1950s that Texas Banking Commissioner Jim Falkner, already saddled with industry problems, called for a separate commissioner to oversee S & Ls. Before this would become a reality, Falkner and the entire state financial community were shaken by an unexpected legal development.

In a case that would bring to the industry the issue of the extent of the banking commissioner's authority, Southwestern S & L, in 1954, notified Falkner's office that it intended to open six branch offices throughout the Houston area.[32] But Falkner refused to act on Southwestern's application, maintaining that it possessed no authority to either approve or disapprove the establishment of branch offices.[33]

Southwestern S & L proceeded anyway, and on September 1, 1956, opened a branch office.[34] The Texas attorney general responded to this by advising the commissioner that approval by the commissioner was a prerequisite to the establishment and operation of an S & L branch office.[35] On January 19, 1958, a state trial court held that there existed neither statutes nor valid regulations, promulgated by the Building and Loan section of the Finance Commission, prohibiting the opening of branch offices without prior approval by the commissioner.[36]

Two years later, however, this decision was overturned, as the Texas Court of Appeals ruled that authority contained in *Vernon's Annotated Texas Statutes* gave the commissioner authority to establish branch offices. The court held that, though not expressed as such, the power was nevertheless implied.[37]

As it turned out, Commissioner Falkner allowed Southwestern S & L to establish branches as it wished, but the importance of the case should not be underestimated. The Court of

Appeals' decision made it clear that state S & Ls differed from state commercial banks. This prompted Falkner to request the creation of the position of Texas savings and loan commissioner. The new commissioner, he hoped, would handle problems peculiar to S & Ls alone—thereby allowing the banking commissioner additional time, and resources, to deal with matters directly concerning the state banking industry.

In reaction to these events the 1961 (fifty-seventh) Texas Legislature passed House Bill 91, which amended Texas Banking Code in the following manner.

An Act amending Article 342-205 of the Texas Banking Code of 1943, same being Acts of the Forty-eighth Legislature, Chapter 97, page 127, et seq., as amended, by creating a Savings and Loan Department; authorizing the appointment of a Savings and Loan Commissioner, a Deputy Savings and Loan Commissioner, and Savings and Loan Examiners, prescribing their qualifications and duties; fixing the conditions under which the rule-making power of the Building and Loan Section of the Finance Commissioner shall be exercised; abolishing the office of Building and Loan Supervisor; relieving the Banking Commissioner of certain duties; and declaring an emergency.[38]

Finally, on September 1, 1961, R. A. Benson was appointed Texas' first savings and loan commissioner. James Gerst, his immediate successor, referred to Benson's appointment—or, more precisely, the appointment of a commissioner per se—as the "emancipation of the Texas savings and loan industry."[39] As we shall see very shortly, Gerst's observation was not without considerable justification.

THE NEW S & L CODE

In the early 1960s control of the Texas S & L industry was fragmented, moving away from control by the state Banking Commission and in the direction of self-regulation. Many industry officials felt this was the perfect opportunity to establish a new S & L code via the Texas Legislature, as they strongly believed that the 1929 code was outdated.[40] Specifically, the predepression code seemed inadequate during periods of rapid industry growth. Loan ceiling limits that were adequate for the 1930s were not nearly high enough for the 1960s.

Another major problem with the 1929 code was that it restricted branching. Consequently, industry officials, led by William G. Richards, chairman of the Legislative Committee of the Texas Savings and Loan League, and Clint Small, Sr., general counsel for the League, were finally moved to draft a new preliminary S & L code, and submit it to the Texas Legislature.[41] Throughout 1962 top S & L officials in the state collaborated with Richards and Small,[42] and by 1963 the Legislature had debated and approved Article 852A, which would become known as the Texas Savings and Loan Act.[43]

To Texas state-chartered thrifts, passage of this act was cause for celebration. Most importantly, the new law granted very liberal rule-making authority to the state industry itself. Indeed, in two sections of Article 852A, *Vernon's Annotated Civil Statutes*, rule-making power is addressed. First, Section 504 states:

. . . promulgate such rules and regulations in respect to loans by associations operating under this law as may be reasonably necessary to assure that such loans are in keeping with sound lending practices and promote the purposes of this Act; provided that such rules and regulations shall not prohibit an association from making any loan or investment that a Federal association could make under applicable Federal regulations.

In Section 11.10, the law states:

Initiation of Rule-Making by Associations. When as many as twenty percent (20%) of the associations subject to this Act petition the Commissioner in writing requesting the promulgation, amendment or repeal of a rule or regulation the Commissioner shall initiate rule-making proceedings. . . .

The net result of this newly realized rule-making power was the effective transfer of Texas S & L governance to the three members of the Building and Loan Section of the Finance Commission and the S & L commissioner. That is, from 1963 until 1984 (when a new state S & L code was adopted) these four individuals could pass regulations without legislative approval.

And they did just that: in 21 years, for every new state law concerning state-chartered S & Ls, approximately seven rule changes were enacted by the Finance Commission's Building and Loan Section.[44]

Furthermore, the 1963 code granted state-chartered S & Ls all new and existing powers granted federally chartered institutions, as seen in Section 1.16 of the code:

Enlargement of Powers: Any provisions of this Act to the contrary notwithstanding, any association may make any loan or investment which such association could make were it incorporated and operating as a Federal association domiciled in this State.[45]

In response to the new S & L code, over the next 12 years all but one new Texas-based S & L was established with a state charter. This trend, and the independence now taken for granted by so many thrifts statewide, provided the setting for extraordinary innovation in S & L operations. This era of innovation is explored in Chapter 4.

NOTES

1. Insolvency is defined as a situation in which the total liabilities of a firm are larger than the firm's total assets, making the net worth of the firm negative.

2. The diversity-risk trade-off is an important factor in forming any portfolio. One way to decrease risk is to have a variety of funds in one's portfolio. This diversity lowers the overall risk involved in investing. With S & Ls having a large portion of their assets in one form, that being home mortgages, the risk factor in their portfolio becomes very high.

3. Prior to 1982 most Savings and Loan Associations were not permitted to invest in assets outside of home mortgages, Federal Home Loan Bank stock, and U.S. government bonds.

4. Most prominent among these are the Federal National Mortgage Association (Fannie Mae), the Government National Mortgage Association (Ginnie Mae), and the Federal Loan Mortgage Corporation (Freddie Mac).

5. The problem of liquidity can go beyond the lack of availability of secondary markets. For example, if an S & L is holding a mortgage

within a low interest rate and wants to sell it, in the secondary market, during a period of high interest rates it may not be able to afford the discount necessary in order to sell the mortgage. The situation in which the S & L cannot afford to sell the loan at a discount leaves the institution in an illiquid position.

6. Geographical lending limitations set on S & Ls by federal and state laws prevent competition in the S & L industry. Without such limitation more associations would be vying for the home mortgage loan business in each area, with the likely result being lower interest rates on home mortgages.

7. *FSLIC-Insured Savings and Loan Associations Combined Financial Statements*, 1950 and 1960 (Washington, D.C: Federal Home Loan Bank Board).

8. *1961 Savings and Loan Fact Book* (Chicago: United States Savings and Loan League, 1961), pp. 7–49.

9. 1949 National Housing Act.

10. *1983 Savings and Loan Source Book* (Chicago: United States League of Savings Associations, 1983), p. 52.

11. H. Morton Bodfish (ed.), *History of Building and Loan in the United States* (Chicago: United States Building and Loan League, 1931), p. 186.

12. Jack Cashin, "History of Savings and Loan Associations in Texas," Doctoral Dissertation, The University of Texas, 1955, p. 187.

13. *Ibid.*, p. 197.

14. *Ibid.*, p. 199.

15. Security Federal Savings and Loan Association of Alice, Texas, was the only Texas S & L to pay any corporate income taxes between the years 1951 and 1963.

16. Josephine Ewalt, *A Business Reborn: The Savings and Loan Story, 1930–1960* (Chicago: American Savings and Loan Institute Press, 1962), p. 265.

17. *Ibid.*

18. *Ibid.*, p. 266.

19. *Ibid.*, p. 268.

20. *Ibid.*, p. 269.

21. *1962 S & L Fact Book*, p. 53.

22. *1966 S & L Fact Book*, p. 98.

23. Political subdivisions refers to governmental jurisdiction areas such as cities and counties.

24. *1965 S & L Fact Book*, p. 70.

25. One basis point is equivalent to one-hundredth of a percentage point. Therefore, a one hundred basis point change in interest is equal to a 1 percent change in the interest rate.

26. *1965 World Almanac and Book of Facts* (New York: New York World Telegram, 1965), p. 254.

27. Edward Williams, *Prospects for the Savings and Loan Industry to 1975* (Austin: Texas Savings and Loan League, 1968), p. 49.

28. *Ibid.*, p. 56.

29. In 1976 the Federal Home Loan Bank Board passed a law that, for the first time, allowed federally chartered S & Ls to have either a stock form of ownership or mutual form of ownership.

30. During the 1950s, Texas state-chartered S & Ls were allowed to make secured loans, up to $500 in areas not related to housing mortgages. These privileges were not available to federally chartered S & Ls.

31. *General and Special Laws of the State of Texas, 41st Legislature, 2nd and 3rd Called Sessions, 1929* (Austin: A. C. Baldwin and Sons, State Printers, 1929), p. 100.

32. *Southwestern Savings and Loan Association of Houston, Texas (Petitioner) v. J. M. Falkner, Banking Commissioner of Texas (Respondent), South Western Reporter*, second series, 331 S.W. 2d 42 (St. Paul: West Publishing Co., 1960), pp. 917–924.

33. *Ibid.*, p. 920.

34. *Ibid.*

35. *Ibid.*, p. 923.

36. *Ibid.*, p. 924.

37. *General and Special Laws of the State of Texas, 48th Legislature, Ch. 97, Subchapter I, Article 342–114, Vernon's Civil Statutes of the State of Texas*, Articles 201 to 578, p. 601.

38. *General and Special Laws of the State of Texas, 57th Legislature, Chapter 198, Article 342–250, Vernon's Civil Statutes of the State of Texas*, Articles 201 to 578, p. 613.

39. Interview with James Gerst, second S & L commissioner of Texas, Austin, March 21, 1986.

40. The 1929 savings and loan code was perceived by most S & L personnel as outdated. It was not specific enough to handle the problems facing S & Ls in the 1950s and 1960s. The code was amended on occasion but industry personnel felt a new code would better guide the Texas S & Ls into the future.

41. The idea for the preliminary 1963 S & L code came basically from William Richards. Mr. Richards sought the express help of Clint Small, Sr. to be sure the wording of the code was in compliance with the banking and S & L laws of Texas.

42. Meetings on the drafting of the 1963 S & L code were not formal and were not scheduled on a regular basis. Whenever possible, meet-

ings were scheduled at a time when most interested S & L personnel were available.

43. *General and Special Laws of the State of Texas, 58th Legislature, 1963, Article 852A,* Texas Savings and Loan Act, p. 269.

44. During the period 1963 to 1984, approximately 85 percent of the rule changes were enacted without passing through the Texas Legislature. Prior to passage of the revised code in 1984, several people were instrumental in determining the operation of state S & Ls. On November 15, 1963, Ray Balsen, Jr., Lacy Bogges, and H. T. Latham (all members of the Building and Loan Section of the Finance Commission), along with R. A. Benson, Texas S & L commissioner, adopted the first set of rules and regulations, under the 1963 revised code, for state-chartered institutions. These are included in *Rules and Regulations for Texas Savings and Loan Associations,* promulgated and adopted November 15, 1963.

45. *General and Special Laws of the State of Texas, 58th Legislature, 1963, Article 852A,* Texas Savings and Loan Act, p. 269.

4

A Framework for Change: The Savings and Loan Industry, 1966–78

The years 1966–78 represented challenge and change for the U.S. savings and loan industry. Developments in the national economy—then record-setting inflation, large increases in the money supply, and rising interest rates—prompted the industry to experiment with new techniques in the arrangement of their assets and liabilities. These techniques were essential to the industry's survival, as without them hundreds of institutions across the United States would have faced insolvency. Moreover, for all S & Ls these new asset and liability powers promised renewed hope for the continuation of their primary function: individual home financing.

In this chapter we experience, first, changes in the national economic landscape and consequent changes in S & L regulation nationwide. Second, we explore the unique history of Texas state-chartered S & Ls during these years, and the way these institutions reacted to problems spawned by the volatile economy.

In order to fully appreciate the magnitude of industry change during these years, it is necessary to understand the place of S & Ls in the U.S. economy, as well as the impact of many factors on their operations. As with all industries, no single event or development spurred immediate, large-scale change for U.S. S & Ls. Instead, many factors accounted for this change. These included legal and regulatory changes enacted by the state and federal governments, competition within the housing-related industries, public—particularly consumer—pressure, technological innovations, and changing economic and market conditions.[1]

Among these factors, legal and regulatory changes stand out as the most uneven. This is because our nation's dual banking system exists within the federal system. As such, the individual states are able to enact legislation as they see fit (provided such legislation does not conflict with federal law). Prior to the 1960s state regulatory structure had limited impact on S & Ls, as their operations were directed mostly by national laws and regulations. By 1966, however, several states—most notably Texas and California—recognized the need for legal and regulatory changes at the state level, and so instituted a series of reforms. Their efforts were followed by similar reforms in other states. As such changes were implemented, the role of government was complicated by the number and diversity of actors involved. That is, within each of the states, and at the national level, there are executive, legislative, regulatory, and judicial participants, as well as outside participants attempting to influence their decision making; this multitude of participants—part of the price of democracy—often creates confusion for those seeking to follow the path of reform.

Equally confusing are the housing-related industries, which feature multiple dimensions. With over 40,000 financial institutions in the United States, including S & Ls, mutual savings, commercial banks, and credit unions, these related industries—homebuilders, realtors, and housing manufacturers—have a direct stake in the home-financing market. But the relationship between financial institutions and their support industries is symbolic; and their mutual reliance commonly creates ripple effects, as occurred in the early 1960s.

The public has often been identified as the forgotten actor in the process of change. Whether this has or has not been true in the past, it can no longer be the case in the future. The consumer is deeply involved as both borrower and saver in the financial world, although these perspectives often compete. Although it may be unclear as to who actually represents the consumer, there is no question that the consumer is having a more prominent impact in Washington as well as in the states. At present this impact is still relatively small, but the influence will continue to grow, and rightly so.

Technology has been another impetus for S & L change, and in the long run it may prove the most important one. For example, as changes have occurred in the technology of electronic funds transfer, critically important innovations have followed, some of which have altered the financial world's balance of power. While government intervention may be marshalled to help resist such alteration, creative innovation can be expected to continue at a rapid pace.

Finally, numerous economic factors and changes in financial markets influence industry reform. The most demonstrable evidence of this is the industry's reaction to rising inflation and interest rates that began in the 1960s. Such conditions, of course, create an unfavorable environment for financial institutions that "borrow short" and "lend long." As the public has become more sophisticated, new financial instruments have been developed and the competition for the market share of consumer savings has intensified. Such economic and market factors provide a constant backdrop and motivation for innovation.[2]

Together, these five factors combine to spur S & L change, in varying degrees depending upon time and circumstances. With this in mind, let us proceed with an examination of the U.S. S & L industry during the 1966–78 era.

U.S. S & Ls: 1966–78

By 1966 the post–World War II era of U.S. S & L activity was over; it ended—like it began—because of dramatically altered economic conditions. Among the most serious problems confronting thrifts by the mid-1960s was the rapid and steep rise in short-term rates. (Indeed, this sharp rise in short-term rates

represented a problem that continues to plague the industry.)
As a result, S & Ls found themselves in the unenviable position of paying rising deposit rates, in order to avoid the loss of
their deposits.

Besides the interest-rate dilemma, thrifts faced serious problems caused by three other developments. First, by the mid-
1960s most commercial banks had begun issuing certificates of
deposit and were aggressively competing for consumer deposits.[3] Second, government agencies began issuing securities that
were, to consumers, far more attractive than they previously
had been. Finally, with the national economy in such turmoil
depositors had become much more conscious of interest rates
than in the past.[4]

In 1965, following two decades of relative price stability, the
United States entered a period marked by spiraling inflation.
That same year, the national economy approached full employ-
ment, a condition that normally prompts governments to exercise restraint in their fiscal and monetary policies. However,
the second half of the 1960s was characterized by decreasing
levels of constraint by the national government. Consequently,
the country's economic expansion—which preceded the government's stepped-up intervention—was accompanied by
speedy, sharp increases in the price of goods and services. Indeed, by 1970 the GNP deflator[5] had climbed by 22 percent
during the preceding five years.[6]

Not unlike most periods of rising prices, the 1960s inflationary era began with a dramatic increase in war-related expenditures. While this provided the initial inflationary spark, the fire
was fueled most generously by a huge expansion of the nation's money supply, which rose steadily from 1961 until 1966—
fully a year after the first signs of runaway inflation had appeared.[7]

It was not until early 1966 that the national government, via
the "Fed," took positive action to curb rising prices. It did so
by severely restricting the money supply. This action, supported by many economists and opposed by others, was a rare
step, so rare that many analysts actually labeled it an "experiment."[8]

In the meantime, money markets continued to tighten, due

largely to the sharp, sporadic rise in most interest rates.[9] In reaction, the FHLBB, fearing that rate competition among S & Ls and commercial banks would result in the failure of many S & Ls, moved to halt the competitive furor. The Board (FHLBB) did this by eliminating, with few exceptions, expansion advances by District Banks[10] to S & Ls paying rates in excess of 4.25 percent on savings accounts.[11] This move, expected to produce quick results, proved largely ineffective.

Still bent on stemming what it viewed as unhealthy competition, the FHLBB next tried interest-rate stabilization. To do so, it successfully lobbied Congress to pass the 1966 Interest Rate Adjustment Act. This law empowered the Board to set interest-rate ceilings for thrifts and to confer with the Federal Reserve Board and the Federal Deposit Insurance Corporation in order to coordinate the ceilings for banks (set by Regulation Q) and thrifts. The idea was to allow thrifts higher ceilings—or what now is commonly called an "interest-rate differential."[12] The coordination would formally be handled through a newly created Interagency Coordinating Committee.

Worth noting is that, prior to 1966, the FHLBB had on many occasions urged Congress to pass this very legislation, without success. However, this is understandable when one fact is taken into account: prior to 1966 its leaders had become supporters. Why? Because by the mid-1960s S & Ls recognized the reality of stiff bank competition and the potential advantage of an interest-rate differential.[13] Still, the legislation was widely regarded—particularly by S & L leaders—as a temporary measure, as it included a provision terminating, within one year, the Board's power to set ceilings.

As it turned out, however, when the expiration date for the Board's rate-setting authority approached, the S & L industry backed off, requesting that Congress extend the Board's authority. The reason for the industry's turnaround was a fear of another tight-money environment by 1968. Congress agreed and eventually made the Board's authority permanent. This delighted S & L industry officials who, in time, came to realize the benefits of such regulation. That is, the FHLBB, in determining rate ceilings, eliminates approximately one-half of the recurring decisions that thrifts would otherwise be forced to make; and this is done without the accompanying fear of disastrous results, as their competitors—banks—are likewise precluded from making decisions about ceilings.[14]

The original structure of the newly imposed rate ceilings was quite simple: passbook accounts were limited to a 4.75 percent rate, while the rate for $1,000-minimum certificates, with 180-day maturities, was fixed at 5.25 percent. However, many times during the 1970s these ceilings were raised and the types of certificates available to consumers increased in number. At the same time, the interest-rate differential between the ceilings on S & L deposits and commercial bank deposits was narrowed. Initially the differential was set at 75 to 100 basis points; by 1970 it was down to 50 basis points, 25 points by 1973, and finally, in 1975, Congress gave the Board authority to eliminate the differential on all categories of accounts.[15]

Passage of the Interest Rate Adjustment Act was followed by a fall in market interest rates (caused, mainly, by an increase in money stock that, during the first three quarters of 1967, grew at an average annual rate of 8.2 percent).[16] Inasmuch as it had been the rise in interest rates that created such problems for thrifts, the drop in rates—and the subsequent return to thrift profitability—might seem to suggest that the industry was saved by the imposition of ceilings. Such a notion is dispelled, however, through an examination of the credit crunches of 1969, 1973, and 1979. These crises showed that whenever market rates surpass existing ceiling rates, disintermediation will occur.

Another important law passed by Congress in 1966 was the Financial Institutions Supervisory Act, which granted the FHLBB authority to issue new "cease-and-desist" orders. These orders, which would take immediate effect, eliminated the ability of the affected S & L to tie up the Board in court.[17]

While this law provided the Board a very broad grant of power, the S & L industry nevertheless was supportive of its passage, for two important reasons. First, the FHLBB, in the early 1960s, began issuing a series of regulations to minimize the possibility of S & L bankruptcies caused by poor management. These regulations, while perhaps responsible for saving a few institutions, at the same time hindered the flexibility of well-run S & Ls. So, industry leaders thought, a cease-and-desist power would enable the FHLBB to act directly to control troubled institutions, thereby eliminating the need for additional regulations, and providing the Board incentive to repeal some of the existing regulations. Second, the healthy S & Ls had long been concerned that the failure of some institutions would generate public unrest about the entire industry, and cause a run on all S & Ls.[18]

The next significant piece of legislation passed by Congress, in 1968, was the Housing and Urban Development Act. This gave federally chartered thrifts the ability to lend for purchases of housing fixtures and mobile trailer homes, and the authority to issue a wide variety of savings plans, notes, bonds, and debentures.[19] (This act led to the creation of the Department of Housing and Urban Development [HUD] which, arguably, represents one of the most significant post–World War II changes in the government's role in the housing and mortgage markets.)[20]

While Congress moved ambitiously to assist financial institutions in their struggles, the FHLBB likewise attempted to help. One thing the Board did was expand the lending capability of S & Ls, by granting them the authority to make both educational loans and investments in urban development projects, and by broadening their authority with respect to apartment lending.[21]

Still trying to manipulate the housing and mortgage markets, the FHLBB in August 1968 lowered the liquidity requirement, from 7 percent to 6.5 percent, and expanded the definition of liquid assets. The change in the percentage rate represented only the second such alteration of its kind since the liquidity requirements were established in 1950.[22] The new definition of "liquid assets" added such things as federal funds, reverse purchase agreements ("repos"), and municipals to assets represented by cash and government securities (already considered liquid).[23]

These changes were significant in that they marked the beginning of a vigorous effort to control liquidity levels and, consequently, the amount of mortgage-lending possible. Indeed, during the decade following the Board's initial liquidity move, 16 additional changes in liquidity requirements—including an especially significant change in January 1972, which left the overall liquidity requirement intact while imposing a short-term requirement—were approved by the Board.[24]

Not to be upstaged by the FHLBB, Congress, in 1969, passed the Tax Reform Act, which jolted the S & L industry by substantially increasing the tax liability of thrifts. Specifically, the law—which in its entirety was directed nationally, not at financial institutions in particular—reduced the allowable additions to loss reserves, from 60 percent of net income to 40 percent.[25] In that same year Congress increased the coverage on insured savings accounts, from $15,000 to $20,000. While this appeared to be only a minor change, the $5,000 increase spurred further increases that, in the 1980s, created big problems for the nation's S & Ls.

Not all developments of importance to S & Ls in the 1960s were of the legal or regulatory variety. One move benefiting the industry was the appointment of Preston Martin as chairman of the FHLBB in 1969. With his appointment the Board underwent an immediate shift in policy, making advances more attractive to the industry, thus stimulating lending.[26] Also during his first year in office, Martin had the Board send questionnaires to industry members, soliciting information about their interest in different types of advances. As might have been expected, the survey results strongly supported a move toward longer term advances. At the time of the survey, the longest consolidated obligation outstanding had a maturity of slightly over two years.[27]

Beyond Martin's appointment, 1969 was marked by the completion of a Board-financed study of the industry, authorized by Congress. Initially, President Lyndon Johnson proposed the study in response to the high rate of growth enjoyed by the S & L industry and the tight-money problems encountered three years earlier.[28] Many of the recommendations emerging from this study would, during the decade following, become policy.

A year later, in 1970, the S & L industry was hit with another sweeping legislative measure, the Emergency Home Finance Act. This law singled out the banking industry as the principal vehicle for President Richard Nixon's plan to revive the nation's depressed housing industry. Four provisions of the act were of greatest importance to thrifts. First, the Federal National Mortgage Association would be permitted to purchase conventional mortgages. Second, the Federal Home Loan Mortgage Corporation (FHLMC), commonly referred to as "Freddie Mac," was created primarily for the purpose of facilitating the development of a secondary market for conventional mortgages. Third, the Board was authorized to offer below-market interest-rate loans, totaling $250 million, provided the funds were used for loans by low- and middle-income families. Finally, the law extended from 20 to 30 years the time given newly created S & Ls to meet net worth requirements.[29]

The net impact of the 1970 act was to liberalize thrifts, offering them fresh hope for the future. In addition, by that time a new advance policy had been initiated, whereby FHLBs were offering loan commitments on a fee basis, and were further providing interested S & Ls the option of securing fixed-rate as well as variable-rate advances. Under the new system long-term advances allowed for early repayments, and prepayments on variable-rate advances were permitted without penalty (though penalties remained for prepayments on fixed-rate advances).[30] To further encourage the use of advances, the Board increased the limit on expansion advances that any single member could acquire, from 17.5 percent to 25 percent of savings deposits, and removed restrictions prohibiting the use of advances for various purposes—-most notably loan acquisitions—outside of an institution's normal concerns.[31]

In addition to these important shifts in matters regarding advances, by 1970 a series of regulatory changes made it possible for S & Ls to issue more than ten different types of accounts— a radical departure from the age-old system of standard, conservative plans. The various accounts would offer differing maximum interest rates, different minimum-balance requirements, and a range of terms over which accounts must be held in order to earn maximum interest.

Among the most significant of these S & L innovations was that permitting institutions to issue variable-rate and split-rate passbook accounts, in addition to their regular passbook account, which is issued without restrictions on term or minimum balance. Besides appealing to the bargain-conscious consumer, these new accounts excited many S & L officials as well. For savers, they offered the advantage of interest rates exceeding those on regular passbook accounts (though none could exceed 5 percent); for S & Ls not paying the regulatory maximum on passbook accounts, these variations allowed them to compete with additional plans.[32]

Another important change in thrifts' savings accounts was the two-year certificate. Not only did this new account in itself represent a sweeping reform in savings practices, but it was the beginning of a trend that led to deposit-rate regulation in the 1970s. Such regulation can be characterized by three distinct patterns. First, a steady increase in the interest-rate differentials between certificate and passbook accounts, whereby increases in the maturity of the certificates accompanied increases in interest-rate differentials. Second, a move (by the end of the decade) to variable-rate ceiling certificates (whose precursor, the so-called wild card account,[33] was introduced in 1973). The third and final pattern was one of extremely sluggish ceiling adjustments, once new ones were in place. For example, in 1970 the passbook ceiling was moved to 5 percent. Three years later it was raised to 5.25 percent; and the next increase, to 5.5 percent, did not come until 1979.[34]

The era of S & L reform was hardly limited to internal changes regarding borrowing, lending, and advance practices. Indeed, by the early 1970s such reform had become a major political concern, in Washington as well as in many state capitals. Thus in 1971 the President's Commission on Financial Structure and Regulation, known as the Hunt Commission, presented its conclusions on the state of U.S. financial institutions. The Hunt study represented, basically, an effort by the federal government to mold the nation's financial system into one that would, in the words of the commission's chairman, "efficiently and equitably serve the financial needs of the country in the coming decades."[35]

The Hunt report, while not providing the immediate reform so many desired, nevertheless, sparked a series of key changes in the years following its release.[36] However, most of these changes would not become law until nearly a decade later, with passage of the 1980 Depository Institutions Deregulation and

Monetary Control Act (DIDMCA), as we shall see in Chapter 5. Even before then the Hunt findings were used to justify numerous attempts at regulatory and legislative reform, most notably the Financial Institutions Act (FIA) of 1973, which the Senate passed but the House of Representatives did not consider.[37] The FIA's reforms, many of which finally became law several years later, with passage of the DIDMCA, included the phasing out of interest-rate ceilings and the interest-rate differential and the granting to institutions of increased lending authority and the ability to offer many additional financial services to consumers.[38]

Even without government-sponsored reform, however, U.S. S & Ls were, by the early 1970s, making important changes from within. Indeed, by this time S & L officers were aggressively competing for business—in sharp contrast to their routine activities of the 1950s and 1960s. This competition included a struggle for FHA mortgages (which many thrifts were by then offering), sales of certificates, merger activities, new branch openings, tinkering—through origination sales, and servicing—with mortgage portfolios, and increasing their use of advances.[39]

Simply stated, by the 1970s flexibility, innovation, and profitability were the thrift industry's new catchwords. At the same time, regulatory activity followed two conflicting modes. One of these was the continual relaxation of rules affecting asset and liability powers; the other was an increase in consumer-oriented directives. As an example of the "relaxation" trend, the Board in 1971 expanded the primary lending territory for an S & L, from an area within the state and within a 100-mile radius of the home office to an area within the state and within a 100-mile radius of any office or branch. The Board went even further, though, approving regulations that eased the method of computing the Federal Insurance Reserve (FIR) requirement, by extending the computation of the deposit base to an average of the three most recent years and giving S & Ls the authority to make, with certain restriction, 95 percent conventional loans.[40]

How did these sweeping changes in laws, regulations, and internal practices affect the industry's performance? Clearly, the early reports were encouraging. That is, while the nation experienced its first bout with stagflation (economic stagnation combined with inflation) of the 1970s, the thrift industry was booming. Indeed, it appeared to most industry analysts that the new rules regarding asset and liability powers were working particularly well, helping the industry grow and prosper. Thus the euphoria S & L leaders experienced in the 1950s had returned—and the dreadful tight-money crisis of the 1960s was long forgotten.

Without question, the primary thrust for S & L revival was provided by the FHLBB, which acted decisively to aid the industry. Most importantly, the Board modified its reserve regulations. As it recognized the difficulty institutions were having in meeting benchmark requirements, the Board simply altered its own requirements. First, in anticipation that savings inflows would taper off late in 1971, the FHLBB suspended reserve allocations. This, Board members believed, would make it easier for many thrifts to meet the established requirements. Then, when savings flow did *not* slow appreciably, the Board modified its method of computing the amount of savings against which the benchmark reserve percentage had to be applied. This modification gave institutions the option of using a three-year average closing savings balance—instead of the single, current-year balance—in computing the required level of reserves. Finally, as savings inflows continued to accelerate in 1972, the Board eased the insurance reserve requirements, offering thrifts a new method for computing net worth.[41]

All told, this relaxation of requirements allowed the S & L industry to grow, by 1972, to the nation's second largest financial intermediary industry, exceeded in total assets only by commercial banks.[42]

The FHLBB's assistance did not, however, end with these reforms. Indeed, in 1973–74, when the thrift industry was jolted by a severe credit crunch, causing market rates to rise well above the regulated ceilings, the Board once again came to the rescue. Without this help the industry faced a crisis of huge proportions, as market rates soared so high that, in many instances, consumers benefited by withdrawing funds and reinvesting—notwithstanding the penalties that accompanied such early withdrawals.[43]

The Board in 1973 responded to this market turbulence by, first, authorizing thrifts to issue two and one-half and four-year certificates, along with the option of offering subordinated debentures (a debenture with a claim on repayment that is inferior to other debentures) and capital notes with a minimum denomination of $50,000 and a minimum maturity of seven years. The Board further increased from 5 percent to 10 percent the percentage of savings that S & Ls could possess in large certificates paying more than 4.75 percent.[44] Also, on these separate occasions in 1973 the FHLBB increased the rate ceiling. Finally, perhaps the most significant innovation of the year came with adoption of the aforementioned "wild card" experiment, which involved removal of the interest-rate ceiling on "jumbo" certificates of deposit, at both S & Ls and commercial banks.[45] (Another important step taken by the Board in 1973, though it affected only New Hampshire and Massachusetts thrifts, was its adoption of regulations permitting the issuing of Negotiable Order of Withdrawal [NOW] accounts.)[46]

In addition to assisting thrifts with their liabilities, the FHLBB offered adjustments for asset procedures that worked to their collective advantage. First, in March 1973, the Board expanded the ability of S & Ls to purchase participation certificates. Three months later it increased the maximum available loan-to-value ratio on construction loans. Then, in September, the Board increased the list of allowable activities for service corporations, and expanded the primary lending area to the entire state (from the earlier 100-mile radius). Finally, in October, the Board authorized the FHLBs to accept deposits paying daily interest, and to accept short-term certificates of deposit; it further permitted thrifts to participate in a program in which they could invest in the federal funds markets.[47]

Obviously 1973 was a year of dramatic change for the nation's thrift industry, especially with respect to government regulation. But it is important to note that the reforms, all of which were permissive, not restrictive, in nature, together represented an important step in the direction of industry deregulation. This was the result of the FHLBB's realization that the industry needed a fresh start—and deregulation, though a gamble, seemed worth a try.

While the Board promoted S & L innovation in 1973, the following year saw the federal government take the lead. In doing so, the national legislature initiated an era of consumer-oriented directives. Indeed, during 1974 Congress passed the Housing and Community Development Act (HCDA), the Employee Retirement Income Security Act (ERISA), the Depository Institutions Amendments (DIA), the Real Estate Settlement Procedures Act (RESPA), and the Equal Credit Opportunity Act (ECOA). Each of these laws broadened the opportunities for U.S. thrift institutions. The HCDA revised upward the loan limits for federal associations, making more consumers eligible to borrow. The ERISA reduced restrictions on Keogh accounts[48] and created Individual Retirement Accounts (IRAs). The DIA increased insurance coverage on accounts from $20,000 to $40,000, gave the FHLBB enforcement authority over stock associations that was the same as that possessed by the Securities and Exchange Commission, and mandated a phase-out of the FSLIC's secondary reserve. The RESPA provided comprehensive guidelines for loan-closing costs and settlement practices. Lastly, the ECOA prohibited institutions from engaging in credit discrimination on the basis of sex or marital status—a move that, most pointedly, forced thrifts to grant more loans to women.[49]

In May 1974 President Nixon announced a $10.3 billion program to assist the housing industry. Of this, $4 billion would be provided through FHLBBs, and $3 billion through the FHLMC. The FHLBBs' portion was to be distributed in the form of five-year advances at below-market interest rates and given to the member banks at the rate of $500 million per month. The FHLMC share went toward a program of forward commitments to purchase mortgages at below-market rates. Here the intention was to have the S & L charge the borrower a below-market rate and shift the mortgage to the FHLMC. Under this program, if the FHLMC could not borrow the necessary funds from the private market, it was authorized to borrow from the U.S. Treasury.[50]

The following year, 1975, offered a quieter government approach to S & L problems. Much of the reason for this was simply the easing of the credit crunch—by then two years old—

which, naturally, lowered market interest rates below the ceiling rates on certificates. But it is important to note that, while the decline in interest rates was due in part to weakened demand for inventory and capital financing, the government also played a major role; it did so by increasing the nation's money supply (M_3) by 12 percent. Together, these factors kept interest rates low during most of 1975 and 1976.[51]

From a regulatory perspective 1975 was a very quiet year, despite the enactment of a good deal of consumer-oriented legislation. Among the most significant laws passed by Congress were Regulation Q and the Home Mortgage Disclosure Act. The former prohibited the elimination or reduction of the existing interest-rate differential between S & Ls and commerical banks without prior approval by Congress. The latter required certain financial institutions to disclose public information about negotiated mortgage loans.[52]

Also in 1975 the FHLBB offered, through publication, its view of the future of the S & L industry. Its basic theme was that both self-interest and public interest would be well-served as thrifts continued to work toward becoming consumer-finance specialists. Significantly, many of the ideas and proposals offered therein were consistent with those earlier suggested by the Hunt Commission.[53]

On a more practical front, the national S & L industry, though weathering the economic recession of 1974–75 relatively well, realized a drop in income nonetheless. Indeed, despite consistent annual industry increases since 1965, total net income after taxes dropped, from $1.9 billion in 1973 to $1.4 billion in 1975.[54]

The next year, 1976, was a very stable one for most S & Ls nationwide. During the year Congress passed a record seven laws affecting the thrift industry. These were the Real Estate Settlement Procedures Act Amendments, the New England NOW Accounts Act, the Equal Credit Opportunity Act Amendments, the Employee Retirement Amendments, the Housing Authorization Act, the Energy Conservation Standards for New Buildings Act, and the Tax Reform Act.[55]

The Employee Retirement Amendments, along with the aforementioned RESPA Amendments, eased various requirements mandated in the original (RESPA) acts. On the other hand, the ECOA Amendments expanded coverage of the original law designed to equalize credit opportunities. The New England NOW Accounts Act simply extended NOW account authority to previously uncovered New England states. The Tax Reform Act—a mixed blessing for the thrift industry—reduced certain allowable federal income tax deductions for associations and increased the minimum tax rate; but it also liberalized IRA and Keogh account provisions.[56]

While these were the most important legal changes made in 1976, other developments should not be ignored. What occurred was a general expansion of the credit market, one that seemed to be benefiting S & Ls. At the same time, FHLBBs continued to expand services to member associations, with many offering open lines of credit to members, and one even offering overdraft advances.[57]

By mid-1977 the nation's economy was advancing nicely, and many economists believed it was time to tighten monetary policy. The administration of President Jimmy Carter, however, was concerned about what it perceived to be a slack in the economy. Consequently, the government adopted a policy designed to stimulate aggregate demand. This was done, first, by a tax reduction in the 1978 budget (Carter's first)—despite warnings by most economists that such a move would fuel inflation. Indeed, these predictions proved to be on target, as the next three-year period was marked by extremely high inflation and gigantic interest-rate hikes.[58]

The president's refusal to pursue a tight money policy resulted in a market interest rate that, by 1978, had once again surpassed the ceiling rate on certificates. In reaction, the FHLBB on June 1 of that year authorized the first of many money market certificates (MMCs),[59] enabling thrifts to compete vigorously with other financial institutions in the struggle for savers, as their interest-rate yields were quite high.

The first MMC approved by the Board featured a 26-week maturity, a $10,000 minimum deposit, and a yield 25 basis points above the auction yield on current six-month Treasury Bills. At the same time it authorized an eight-year certificate with a $1,000 minimum balance and an 8 percent ceiling. But it was the 26-

week (six-month) maturity period that represented the most fundamental industry shift of the decade. This innovation meant, quite simply, that S & Ls would be forced to offer market rates on at least one form of deposit.[60] But when the six-month option was introduced, many industry leaders balked, convinced it would prove harmful by raising the average cost of institutions' deposits, without providing any tangible benefits. In the final analysis, however, though the cost of funds did rise, MMC accounts proved very helpful (especially to struggling thrifts), as they helped prevent disintermediation. In fact, such accounts became so popular that, in 1981, they represented more than 40 percent of total S & L deposits nationwide.[61]

Also in 1978 the industry was treated to passage of the Financial Institutions Regulatory and Interest Rate Control Act. The most critical provision of this important law was one increasing FSLIC coverage of pension deposits, and other trusted personnel benefit plans, from $40,000 to $100,000.[62] Eventually the $100,000 limit would apply to individual accounts as well, with passage of the 1980 Depository Institutions Deregulation and Monetary Control Act. But it was the 1978 act that paved the way for higher limits across-the-board.

Thus with the help of government deregulation the S & L industry not only weathered the credit crunches of 1966, 1969, and 1973, but proved amazingly resilient. As shown in Table 4.1, the industry experienced tremendous growth in the late 1970s. In 1978 after-tax income for all thrifts reached a record-high level; and 1977 and 1979 were banner years as well.

Of additional significance to S & Ls is return on equity and return on average assets. As revealed in Table 4.2, 1978 again stands out as the industry's best year, with the highest return in both categories. Moreover, industry growth was steady *throughout* the 1966–78 period, as Table 4.3 shows. Indeed, during those years the assets of all FSLIC-insured S & Ls rose more than fourfold, while their collective net worth increased better than threefold. So, despite the gloomy predictions of cynics, the industry did not, during this period of national economic turmoil, face collapse; instead, as measured in net worth, assets, return, and overall growth, the industry flourished.

Without a doubt much of the success enjoyed by S & Ls in

Table 4.1
Statement of Operations of All Savings Associations (millions of dollars)

Year	Operating Income	Operating Expense	Net Operating Income	Net Income Before Taxes	Net Income After Taxes
1965	7,081	1,366	5,715	978	821
1970	11,039	1,969	9,072	1,152	904
1971	13,073	2,180	10,893	1,739	1,291
1972	15,572	2,524	13,048	2,378	1,729
1973	18,692	3,026	15,666	2,729	1,950
1974	21,477	3,490	17,987	2,213	1,532
1975	24,193	3,979	20,214	2,135	1,485
1976	28,878	4,689	24,189	3,294	2,302
1977	34,623	5,443	29,180	4,710	3,268
1978	41,409	6,302	35,107	5,832	3,997
1979	49,554	7,227	42,327	5,299	3,691
1980	57,188	8,068	49,120	1,215	798
1981	66,452	9,155	57,297	-6,271	-4,725
1982	73,278	10,478	62,800	-6,010	-4,264

Sources: Federal Home Loan Bank Board; United States League of Savings Institutions.

the 1970s resulted from legal and regulatory changes enacted by Congress and the FHLBB. That is, growth within the industry clearly coincided with these changes, which are properly characterized as deregulatory. However, as we examine the years following 1978, two things should be kept in mind. First, some of the credit must go to S & L officials, many of whom had for years been recommending the very changes that the national government finally saw fit to enact. Furthermore, it was the courage and foresight of these industry leaders—to act on these new freedoms, despite their inherent risks—that truly accounted for S & L growth in the 1970s. Second, while the government had by 1978 begun dabbling with a relaxation of rules for thrifts, true deregulation of the industry, though just around the corner, had yet to occur.

TEXAS S & Ls: 1963–78

While U.S. thrifts fared well during the 1963–78 period, Texas state-chartered thrifts were at the forefront of industry innova-

Table 4.2
Selected Significant Ratios of Savings Associations

Year	Return on Equity	Return on Average Assets
1965	9.76%	.67%
1970	8.01	.57
1971	10.53	.72
1972	12.15	.79
1973	12.18	.77
1974	8.65	.55
1975	7.85	.48
1976	11.14	.64
1977	13.99	.79
1978	14.91	.84
1979	12.11	.68
1980	2.45	.13
1981	-15.39	-.74
1982	-15.60	-.62

Sources: Federal Home Loan Bank Board; United States League of Savings Institutions.

tion. This innovation fervor came, initially, with an overhaul of
the state's S & L code in 1963. Basically, the industry-prompted
reform gave sweeping authority to the Texas S & L commissioner and the three members of the Building and Loan section
of the Texas Finance Commission, to promulgate and adopt
any rule or regulation they deemed beneficial to the state S & L
industry.[63] Clearly, in the absence of such rule-making power
Texas would not have been in the position to act as leader in
the national thrift industry. Consequently, though passage of
the new code occurred during the era chronicled in Chapter 3,
the reforms contained therein need to be considered in the con-
text of developments during the 1966–78 period; hence, the slight
overlap of S & L eras.

TEXAS AS INNOVATOR

Eager to foster their collective growth, Texas S & Ls were the
first in the United States to engage in commercial loans, consumer loans, and direct real-property investments. This is why,

Table 4.3
Total Liabilities of All Savings Associations (millions of dollars)

Year-End	Net Worth	Total Assets
1965	$ 8,704	$129,580
1970	12,401	176,183
1971	13,592	206,023
1972	15,240	243,127
1973	17,056	271,905
1974	18,442	295,545
1975	19,779	338,233
1976	21,998	391,907
1977	25,184	459,241
1978	29,057	523,542
1979	32,638	578,962
1980	33,391	629,829
1981	28,395	664,167
1982	26,157	706,045

Sources: Federal Home Loan Bank Board; United States League of Savings Institutions.

when the FHLBB urged Congress to pass the DIDMCA and the Garn–St. Germain Act, it pointed to the example set by Texas' pioneer deregulation efforts.[64] Today it is common knowledge that the bolstered powers of federal thrifts, granted them via these two pieces of legislation, were to a great extent patterned after laws already governing Texas state-chartered S & Ls. It is, therefore, useful to consider some of the important freedoms granted, first, to Texas thrifts, and subsequently made available to federal S & Ls (through enactment of the DIDMCA and Garn–St. Germain).

For the first time, the term "personal loan"[65] appeared among the laws and regulations governing Texas S & Ls. Below we see excerpts of the state's revised code covering such loans, made with the blessing of the Texas Finance Commission and the state's Savings and Loan commissioner:

Any association may make personal loans, secured or unsecured, to members, provided the net amount advanced on any such loan does not exceed Five Thousand Dollars ($5,000.00). . . . [66]

In 1965, the rule was changed to read

(A) Any association may make loans, secured or unsecured to members, provided the net amount advanced and outstanding on any such loan or loans to any one member, shall not exceed $5,000.00.

(B) Any association may make other loans to members, adequately *secured* by tangible personal property, provided the net amount advanced and outstanding on all of such loans to any one member does not exceed $7,500.00 or an amount equal to 1% of the Association's net worth, whichever is greater. . . . [67]

The 1965 change permitted secured loans up to $7,500, or 1 percent of an association's net worth, whichever was greater (in many instances, 1 percent of net worth did exceed $7,500).[68] In subsequent years this regulation was amended repeatedly until, on August 3, 1972, Texas state-chartered S & Ls were given the freedom to offer consumer loans with virtually no percentage-of-assets limitations.[69]

On the other hand, federal S & Ls did not receive extended consumer-loan privileges until passage of the DIDMCA and Garn–St. Germain—approximately one decade after their implementation in Texas. Moreover, even when federal institutions were granted such privileges, they were saddled by asset requirements. Specifically, in 1980 (after the DIDMCA's passage), an S & L could feature such loans only so long as they did not amount to more than 20 percent of its total assets; then, in 1982 (with enactment of Garn–St. Germain), the limit on these loans as a percentage of assets was raised to 30 percent.[70]

Just as important to the industry as personal loans were commercial loans, which, in 1963, were for the first time made available by Texas state-chartered S & Ls. Two amendments to Texas law made this possible. The first stated that no association shall

(1) Make a loan on real estate, on which is located or on which from the proceeds of the loan will be located a home or homes or combination of home and business property, that exceeds eighty percent (80%) of the appraised valuation of such real estate plus the value of any savings account in the association or any real estate loan pledged as additional collateral to secure such loan. For the purpose of this

paragraph a home shall mean a dwelling for not more than four (4) families.

(2) Make a loan on real estate other than the type described in (1) above that exceeds sixty-five percent (65%) of the appraised valuation of such real estate plus the value of any additional collateral of the type described in (1) above pledged to secure such loan.[71]

Equally important was another section of the same law, which provided:

Loans Shall Conform to Rules and Regulations of the Commissioner and Building and Loan Section of the Finance Commission. The Commissioner and the Building and Loan Section of the Finance Commission . . . shall, from time to time, promulgate such rules and regulations in respect to loans by associations operating under this law as may be reasonably necessary to assure that such loans are in keeping with sound lending practices and promote the purposes of this. . . .[72]

Together these statutes permitted real estate loans other than the ordinary one- to four-bedroom family home loan, or the typical combination home/business loan. The new loans would be limited to 65 percent of appraised valuation, but the commissioner retained authority to amend this restriction, as well as to promulgate whatever new rules and regulations he deemed necessary. Consequently, beginning in 1963 Texas thrifts rushed to approve loans for the development of shopping centers, warehouses, commercial garages, and other permanent structures.[73]

Once again, however, federal S & Ls had to wait until 1980 to enjoy these extended commercial real estate-loan powers. Even then such authority came with a restriction: such loans could not exceed 20 percent of an institution's total assets. Two years later (under Garn–St. Germain) the restriction was softened, as the limit was increased to 40 percent.[74]

A third critical power—again, realized first by Texas thrifts and much later by their federally chartered counterparts—involved real estate development. In 1967, after viewing with satisfaction the experimentation with personal- and commercial-loan liberalization, the Texas S & L code was amended as follows:

An association may purchase and invest in real property in the course of its business and such investments may include subdividing, developing and improving of the real property, and building homes and other buildings authorized herein shall be designed as facilities for the offering of retail commercial and service uses to the residential occupants in the area of such improvements. An association may own, rent, lease, manage, operate for income, or sell such property. Investments of an association under this section shall not at any one time aggregate more than an amount equal to 50% of the sum of the association's loss reserves, surplus, permanent reserve fund stock and undivided profits, as of the day of the last closing of the association's books prior to the making of such investment.[75]

These freedoms greatly enhanced the growth potential of Texas thrifts, and they were quick to capitalize on that potential.

Eventually—again, beginning in 1980—the federal government granted federally chartered S & Ls these real estate development powers. Not surprisingly, these institutions responded eagerly to this opportunity to expand. However, until January 1985 direct federal S & L investments in real estate were limited to 10 percent of an institution's assets, except in cases where Board approval was granted.[76]

As with these powers first granted to Texas S & Ls and later given to federal thrifts, many other options originated in Texas. For example, while the DIDMCA in 1980 finally authorized federally chartered S & Ls to make unsecured construction loans, such loans were available at Texas state-chartered thrifts as early as 1963. While federal associations in 1980 were given authority to invest in guaranteed national, state, and local obligations, Texas S & Ls were again provided this option 17 years earlier. Finally, in their 1963 liberation Texas thrifts were given the privilege of investing in time and savings deposits of other S & Ls; for federal institutions this authority did not appear until 1982.[77]

In large, structural areas Texas S & Ls also moved more swiftly than those with federal charters. For example, one very significant breakthrough for federal thrifts, granted via Garn–St.

Germain, was a provision permitting them to allocate as much as 30 percent of assets to commercial paper and corporate debt securities. Long before then, however, the revised Texas S & L code gave the state commissioner the power to approve and identify investments in any security or obligation he deemed beneficial to the state's S & Ls. As a result, by the early 1970s— fully a decade before passage of Garn–St. Germain—Texas state-chartered thrifts were investing in commercial paper and corporate debt securities, and profiting therefrom.[78]

Beyond leading the nation's other S & Ls into the 1980s, Texas state-chartered institutions also adopted, during the 1970s and 1980s, various options that only today are being considered at the federal level. For example, in 1974 the Texas S & L code was amended, eliminating the prohibition against state S & Ls offering merchandise as inducements to open new accounts.[79] Even today, the "giveaway" concept has yet to be adopted by federal thrifts.

Another area where federal thrifts continue to lag behind Texas associations is in "raw land" investment.[80] By 1965 Texas law was amended to permit state S & Ls to make loans for raw land.[81] Yet more than two decades later federally chartered S & Ls are barely edging into this lucrative investment area.

While most of the statutes, rules, and regulations governing Texas state-chartered thrifts were adopted in the 1960s and early 1970s, most of these have subsequently been amended, and many times broadened considerably. For example, the provision regarding property-improvement loans was amended nine times between 1963 and 1984.

Although many have questioned the wisdom of Texas' government and S & L industry for having so revolutionized the industry, few doubt the general importance of the leadership role Texas assumed, as it moved by leaps and bounds to save its troubled institutions. This is why, in 1982, the FHLBB formally acknowledged, with a ceremonial plaque, recognition of the efforts of Texas S & L pioneer Alvis Vandygriff (then commissioner of the Texas S & L Department). This was a simple sincere statement of thanks to Mr. Vandygriff, Texas, and the state's S & L industry in general, for providing the leadership and innovation that resulted in a revived thrift industry.[82]

TEXAS S & L GROWTH: 1966–78

During this era of legislative and regulatory shuffling the Texas S & L industry experienced rapid, relatively steady growth. Indeed, while this 12-year period was marked by a 300 percent growth among S & Ls nationwide (as measured in assets, from $128 billion to $510 billion), Texas state-chartered institutions grew by more than 450 percent (from $3.7 billion to $20.7 billion). Significantly, federally chartered thrifts in Texas—subject, of course to the same economic climate as their state-chartered competitors—grew only 270 percent (from $1.9 billion to $7.1 billion), actually less than the national average.[83]

Another telling statistic is the number of active institutions at the beginning and end of this period. In 1966 there were 4,510 S & Ls across the United States. By 1978 the number had fallen to 4,053. Within Texas the decline in federally chartered thrifts was comparable to the national drop (from 87 to 71). Thanks to the liberalization of laws governing Texas state-chartered S & Ls, the number of such institutions increased dramatically, from 180 to 247.[84] This increase was due, specifically, to the passage of laws making possible vastly increased asset potential.

During this period of innovation, consumers, like institutions, benefited. As revealed in Table 4.4, throughout these years S & Ls nationwide offered interest rates above those given at commercial banks. (This resulted, of course, in huge increases in both the assets and liabilities of thrifts.) So the advantages spawned by deregulation of the Texas thrift industry were not restricted to Texas, but were enjoyed by institutions and savers nationwide.

Much of the incentive for Texas S & L innovation was provided by the state's rapid growth. Between 1966 and 1978 the population of Texas increased by more than 24 percent.[85] Consequently, the demand for new homes and apartments rose as well—and the state's S & Ls, now equipped with a variety of exciting options, were more than willing to finance these new structures.

In addition to population growth, the Texas population was growing wealthier. Part of the explanation for this was that the

Table 4.4
Average Annual Yield on Selected Types of Investments

Year	Savings Deposits in Savings Associations	Savings Deposits in Mutual Savings Banks	Time and Savings Deposits in Commercial Banks
1965	4.23%	4.11%	3.69%
1966	4.45	4.45	4.04
1967	4.67	4.74	4.24
1968	4.68	4.76	4.48
1969	4.80	4.89	4.87
1970	5.06	5.01	4.95
1971	5.33	5.14	4.78
1972	5.39	5.23	4.66
1973	5.55	5.45	5.71
1974	5.98	5.76	6.93
1975	6.24	5.89	5.92
1976	6.32	5.98	5.53
1977	6.41	6.03	5.50
1978	6.52	6.14	6.02
1979	7.31	6.85	7.29

Sources: Federal Deposit Insurance Corporation; Federal Home Loan Bank Board; Federal Reserve Board.

state, known as a haven for investments, was attracting many out-of-state investors. Consequently, Texas' state-chartered thrifts were able to make loans in Texas, while selling such loans to other financial intermediaries outside of the state.[86] Indeed, by the end of the 1970s Texas S & Ls were selling nearly one-half of all Texas-based loans to intermediaries located outside of the state.[87] This not only enriched the state's economy, but contributed enormously to the success of its S & Ls as well.

TEXAS S & Ls, 1966–78: A SUMMARY

The period 1966–78 was one in which Texas S & Ls were freed from many of the limitations—especially those involving assets—that continued to saddle federal institutions. With the severe credit crunch of 1966 it became obvious that new, shorter term assets, closely resembling the short-term liability structure of the industry, were needed. But it was only Texas S & Ls that, due to radical legislative reforms, were offered the ability to alter their asset-producing practices.

Still, by 1978 most Texas thrifts were making relatively little use of their new powers. Indeed, by that time these associations had over 82 percent of their assets in fixed-rate, long-term home mortgages.[88] By 1979 new problems confronted the entire S & L industry, and Texas thrifts were forced to rethink their conservative asset practices. In Chapter 5 we will see how S & Ls, in and out of Texas, responded to a fresh crisis.

NOTES

1. *FHLB-San Francisco Second Annual Conference: Change in the Savings and Loan Industry* (San Francisco, 1976), p. 16.

2. *Ibid.*, p. 17.

3. 1962 was the first year federal laws allowed commercial banks to issue certificates of deposit.

4. Dwight M. Jaffee, "What to Do About Savings and Loan Associations?" *Journal of Money, Credit and Banking*, November 1974, p. 540.

5. The GNP deflator is a measure of the price level equal to the ratio of current-year nominal GNP to current-year real GNP times 100. It is the federal government's most commonly used tool to measure inflation.

6. Philip Cagan, *Persistent Inflation—Historical and Political Essays* (New York: Columbia University Press, 1979), p. 97.

7. From 1961 through 1962 the annual growth rate of M_1 did not exceed 3 percent for any six month period. By 1965 this growth rate had more than doubled to over 6 percent.

8. Since 1966, tight monetary policies have been advocated by many, in and out of government, as the cure for an ailing company.

9. Cagan, p. 97.

10. District banks are branches of the U.S. Federal Reserve Banking System. They provide funds for financial institutions seeking to make loans.

11. John M. Buckley, Jr., "The Federal Home Loan Bank Board," *Federal Home Loan Bank Board Journal*, April 1982, p. 5.

12. Walter J. Woerheide, *The Savings and Loan Industry: Current Problems and Possible Solutions* (Westport, Conn.: Quorum Books, 1984), p. 9.

13. *Ibid.*

14. The S & L manager has traditionally had two basic price decisions to make. One is the price paid for deposits, and the other is the price charged for mortgages.

15. Andrew Carron, *The Plight of Thrift Institutions* (Washington, D.C., 1982), p. 5.

16. Cagan, p. 110.

17. *Savings and Loan Fact Book 1978* (Chicago: United States League of Savings Associations, 1978), p. 118.

18. *Ibid.*, pp. 33–34.

19. *Ibid.*, p. 118.

20. Jaffee, p. 541.

21. John E. Home, Statement, *Federal Home Loan Bank Board Journal*, April 1982, p. 79.

22. Woerheide, p. 10.

23. *Ibid.*, p. 11.

24. *Ibid.*

25. *1970 S & L Fact Book*, p. 102.

26. Advances are basically loans from the FHLBB to S & Ls that are generally used to meet new mortgage demand or replace the S & Ls' liquidity lost through the withdrawal of savings.

27. A "consolidated obligation" is a bond sold by the Office of Finance of the FHLBB. The amount and frequency of the sale of consolidated obligations are based on requests by the FHLBs. The proceeds from the sale are distributed to the FHLBs according to their requests.

28. Thomas B. Marvell, *The Federal Home Loan Bank Board* (New York: Praeger, 1969), p. 36.

29. R. Bruce Ricks and Harris C. Friedman, "The Housing Opportunity Allowance Program," *Federal Home Loan Bank Board Journal*, December 1971, p. 6.

30. Preston Martin, "New Credit Policies for the 1970s: A Discussion of FHLBB Objectives," *Federal Home Loan Bank Board Journal*, December 1970, p. 3.

31. *Ibid.*, p. 4.

32. *1971 S & L Fact Book*, p. 65.

33. "Wild card" accounts were certificates on which S & Ls and banks were allowed to pay any rate of interest, provided there was a $1,000 minimum deposit.

34. *1983 Savings and Loan Source Book* (Chicago: United States League of Savings Institutions, 1983), p. 50.

35. Robert Edmister, *Financial Institutions: Markets and Management* (New York: McGraw-Hill, 1980), p. 258.

36. *Ibid.*

37. Kent W. Colton, "Financial Reform: A Review of the Past and Prospects for the Future," invited working paper no. 37, Office of Pol-

icy and Economic Research, Federal Home Loan Bank Board, September 1980, p. 15.

38. Buckley, p. 11.

39. Woerheide, p. 14.

40. *Ibid.* One restriction was that all loans above 80 percent had to have private mortgage insurance, or the S & L had to keep an equivalent amount in its reserves.

41. *1974 S & L Fact Book*, p. 100.

42. *1973 S & L Fact Book*, p. 144.

43. Cagan, p. 179.

44. Prior to 1973, S & Ls were able to issue certificates with 2.5-year and 4.0 year maturities but could not pay a higher yield. The new rules allowed higher yields for these longer maturities.

45. "Jumbo Certificates" are certificates of deposit at commercial banks and S & Ls with a minimum deposit of $100,000.

46. A NOW account is the same as an interest-bearing checking account at a bank.

47. Woerheide, p. 15.

48. Keogh accounts are basically IRA accounts for individuals who are self-employed.

49. Woerheide, p. 15.

50. *Ibid.*, p. 16.

51. Cagan, p. 198.

52. *1983 Savings and Loan Source Book*, p. 52.

53. *A Financial Institution for the Future: Savings, Housing, Finance, Consumer Services: An Examination of the Restructuring of the Savings and Loan Industry*, (Washington, D.C.: Federal Home Loan Bank Board, 1975).

54. *1988 Savings Institutions Source Book*, (Chicago: United States League of Savings Institutions, 1988), p. 50.

55. *1978 S &L Fact Book*, pp. 119–120.

56. *Ibid.*

57. James L. Richter, "Office of the Federal Home Loan Banks," *Federal Home Loan Bank Board Journal*, April 1976, p. 25.

58. Cagan, p. 198.

59. Money market certificates are a type of certificate that allows the interest payment to fluctuate along with market interest rates.

60. Colton, p. 22.

61. *1982 Source Book*, p. 23.

62. *1988 Savings Institutions Source Book*, p. 68.

63. *General and Special Laws of the State of Texas, 58th Legislature, 1963, Article 852A*, Texas Savings and Loan Act, p. 269.

64. Federal Home Loan Bank officials have, on several occasions, cited Texas S & L laws as being instrumental in the writing of the 1982 Garn–St. Germain Act. Alvis Vandygriff, former Texas S & L commissioner, was given a plaque by the FHLBB for his role in structuring Texas S & L laws that served as a model for the Garn–St. Germain Act.

65. Texas S & Ls did offer limited forms of consumer loans as far back as 1929 but it was not until 1963 that the term "Personal Loan" was used in Texas S & L laws.

66. *Chapter 8, Section 4, Rules and Regulations for Texas Savings and Loan Associations*, promulgated and adopted November 15, 1963.

67. *Ibid.*

68. An S & L could lend up to 1 percent of its net worth or $7,500, whichever was greater, to one customer as a personal loan. For many Texas S & Ls the 1 percent of net worth figure was larger than $7,500. So as long as an S & L had net worth of over $750,000, which many S & Ls had, this 1 percent of net worth would be the larger of the two figures.

69. *Rules and Regulations for Texas Savings and Loan Associations*, promulgated and adopted August 3, 1973.

70. *1983 Source Book*, pp. 53–54. The Housing and Urban Development Act of 1968 granted federal associations new limited lending powers. For example, federal associations could make unsecured loans, up to $5,000, to finance equipment that was placed in the home. Loans, up to $5,000, could also be made on "second" or vacation homes. These limited powers were enlarged dramatically with the passage of the 1980 DIDMC Act.

71. *General and Specific Laws of the State of Texas, 58th Legislature, 1963, Article 852A*, section 5.05, Texas Savings and Loan Act, p. 13.

72. *General and Specific Laws of the State of Texas, 58th Legislature, 1963, Article 852A*, section 5.04, Texas Savings and Loan Act, p. 12.

73. Interview with Sales Lewis, Texas S & L commissioner 1967–77, on May 4, 1986.

74. *1983 Source Book*, pp. 53–54.

75. *Rules and Regulations for Texas Savings and Loan Associations*, promulgated and adopted, July 14, 1967.

76. "Divided Bank Board Extends Its Curbs on S & L Holdings, Sets Public Hearing," *Wall Street Journal*, December 19, 1986, p. 46.

77. *General and Specific Laws of the State of Texas, 58th Legislature, 1963, Article 852A*, Texas Savings and Loan Act, p. 269.

78. *General and Specific Laws of the State of Texas, 58th Legislature, 1963, Article 852A*, section 5.11, Texas Savings and Loan Act, p. 16.

79. *Rules and Regulations for Texas Savings and Loan Associations*, promulgated and adopted September 15, 1974.

80. "Raw land" investments are those made by the S & Ls to purchase raw land with the anticipation of developing it for later commercial or residential projects.

81. *Rules and Regulations for Texas Savings and Loan Associations*, promulgated and adopted August 30, 1965.

82. The plaque was awarded to Alvis Vandygriff on December 31, 1982. Mr. Vandygriff was the only commissioner to receive an award from the FHLBB for his leadership role in making Texas a model for the Garn–St. Germain Act.

83. *Fiftieth Annual Report of Texas Savings and Loan Associations*, Texas Savings and Loan Department, Austin, 1978.

84. *Ibid*.

85. *1986–1987 Texas Almanac* (Dallas: A. H. Belo Corporation, 1986), p. 385.

86. A financial intermediary is any financial institution that performs the function of channeling funds from savers to investors. Some of the larger financial intermediaries are commercial banks, S & Ls, life insurance companies, and private pension funds.

87. Interview with Alvis Vandygriff on November 14, 1986.

88. *Fiftieth Annual Report of Texas Savings and Loan Associations*.

5

U.S. S & Ls: 1979–82: The First Crisis of the 1980s

In Chapter 4 we observed that the problems that eventually would shape the S & L industry first appeared in the mid-1960s, and worsened until, by 1979, they represented a potential catastrophe. In this chapter we examine the critical years 1979–82, with an eye both to the national crisis and to that endured by Texas institutions.

NATIONAL S & Ls IN TROUBLE

Many economists argue that the appointment of Paul Volcker as chairman of the Federal Reserve Board in 1979 was the single most important cause of the unraveling of the nation's thrift industry in the 1980s.[1] Volcker, then a confirmed monetarist (i.e., one who believes that movements in the nation's money supply are the primary causes of ups and downs in business activity), believed that the money supply—not interest rates—was the key to controlling runaway inflation (averaging, at his appointment, about 12 percent annually). His method of attack

Table 5.1
Selected Interest Rates, 1976–82

Year	Asset Yield Savings & Loan Associations	Cost of Funds Savings & Loan Associations
1976	8.18	6.38
1977	8.44	6.44
1978	8.73	6.67
1979	9.29	7.47
1980	9.72	8.94
1981	10.11	10.92
1982	10.82	11.38

Source: *Economic Report of the President 1983*, p. 240.

was to restrict the availability of money so as to stabilize prices; interest rates, he believed, would eventually decline. Thus with tight money and declining interest rates, prices naturally should drop.

So Volcker and the Fed acted to restrict the national money supply. This, however, raised the cost of borrowing, via higher interest rates. Indeed, the prime interest rate, which generally provides a fair barometer of other short-term interest rates,[2] reached in 1981 an all-time high—20.5 percent.[3] This in itself constituted an industry-wide crisis for U.S. S & Ls, one of major proportions; but things would get even worse. Following the prime rate's peak, most large investors reached the conclusion that such a rate could not be sustained and acted on their collective belief. The result was what economists call an "inverted yield curve," wherein short-term securities are yielding a return greater than that of longer term securities.[4] This condition, always injurious to the national economy in general, was particularly devastating to the S & L industry. As revealed in Table 5.1, the effect was palpable and immediate.

In examining the period 1976–82, we find that the sudden impact of dramatically increased interest rates produced a horrifying reality for thrifts: by the year 1981 their cost of funds actually exceeded their asset yield! Since there was no margin between short-term deposits and long-term loans, loan origination fees[5] became the primary source of short-run profits on newly written mortgages; they were used, most of the time, simply to pay operating costs.

Across the United States S & Ls were confronted by a two-pronged attack on their deposits. First, for those deposits without rate ceilings, the cost of maintaining the funds caught up with and eventually exceeded the returns on mortgage portfolios (as shown in Table 5.1). Second, those deposits with rate ceilings were being withdrawn at an alarming, unprecedented rate, as rate-conscious S & L customers sought higher yields in the unregulated investment areas like money market mutual funds.[6] This disintermediation created for U.S. thrifts a liquidity crisis, the magnitude of which its leaders could scarcely fathom.

By themselves, these dilemmas were sufficient to rock the S & L industry, but they represented only the beginning of the industry's troubles. The aforementioned tight-money policies adopted by the Fed soon triggered a national recession, spawning the worst housing slide in U.S. history. For the thrift industry, this posed a serious threat: even if the yield curve resumed its normal (upward) shape, the demand for mortgages would prove insufficient to boost asset portfolio yields.[7]

So in order to maintain liquidity sufficient to meet increasing deposit outflows, S & Ls were forced to abandon—liquidate—part of their portfolios in the secondary markets.[8] However, by the time they moved to do so, interest rates had significantly eroded the value of mortgage assets. Since the mortgages were carried at face value, losses on sales were counted against net worth. This phenomenon, coupled with the deteriorating earnings picture, sent many thrift institutions to—and in some cases beyond—the brink of insolvency.[9]

Not surprisingly, this combination of adversities caused industry-wide chaos, in addition to huge financial losses. As seen in Table 5.2, the years 1981–82 by themselves produced S & L after-tax losses of nearly $9 billion. Table 5.3 shows that institutions' return on equity and on average assets[10]—both of which typically reflect profits—for these same two years represented substantial losses. All told, by the end of 1981 many industry analysts estimated that 1,500 or more S & Ls faced imminent

Saving the Savings and Loan

Table 5.2
Statement of Operations of All Savings Associations (millions of dollars)

Year	Net Income Before Taxes	Taxes	Net Income After Taxes
1960	$ 581	$ 4	$ 577
1965	978	157	821
1970	1,152	248	904
1971	1,739	448	1,291
1972	2,378	649	1,729
1973	2,729	779	1,950
1974	2,213	681	1,532
1975	2,135	650	1,485
1976	3,294	992	2,302
1977	4,710	1,442	3,268
1978	5,832	1,835	3,997
1979	5,299	1,608	3,691
1980	1,215	417	798
1981	-6,271	-1,546	-4,725
1982	-6,010	-1,746	-4,264

Sources: Federal Home Loan Bank Board; United States League of Savings Institutions.

liquidation or merger.[11] The industry had reached its proverbial "rock bottom."

THE S & L INDUSTRY IN REACTION

As the plight of S & Ls worsened, industry leaders began looking to legislators and government regulators for help. They were met with fierce resistance, particularly from those favoring free-market economics. Such opponents contended that S & L problems were no more than an indication that the nation's resources were not being used efficiently, and that if the transfer of some resources to efficient areas of the economy meant the collapse of the S & L industry, so be it. These laissez-faire advocates further suggested that, given the existence of deposit insurance, a government bail-out of the industry would mean a windfall for owners of firms actively engaged in mismanagement.[12] Needless to say, this position—on its face

Table 5.3
Selected Significant Ratios of Savings Associations

Year	Profit Margin	Return on Equity	Return on Average Assets
1960	15.44%	12.26%	.87%
1965	11.57	9.76	.67
1970	8.56	8.01	.56
1971	10.26	10.53	.72
1972	11.01	12.16	.79
1973	10.31	12.18	.77
1974	7.03	8.65	.55
1975	6.06	7.85	.48
1976	7.87	11.14	.64
1977	9.32	13.99	.79
1978	9.57	14.91	.84
1979	7.37	12.11	.68
1980	1.38	2.45	.13
1981	-6.96	-15.39	-.74
1982	-5.49	-15.60	-.62

Sources: Federal Home Loan Bank Board; United States League of Savings Institutions.

consistent with the most basic tenets of capitalism—did not please S & L industry officials.

Defenders of the thrift industry countered the free-market argument by asserting, first, that they too preferred open market competition to an arena dominated by government interference. But, they pointed out, this was no time to change the rules of the game. For decades, they argued, S & Ls across the United States had been saddled with limitations on their activities. Therefore, industry spokespeople contended, even if thrifts had, during those years, been of a mind to diversify into a more efficient, competitive mode, legal restrictions would have made such a shift impossible.[13]

Moreover, S & L apologists argued, the industry's crisis was caused not by overt mismanagement, but by the precipitate rise in interest rates.[14] These rate hikes, they pointed out, were spurred by a combination of monetary and fiscal policies undertaken by the national government. Hence, they concluded, this same government should clean up the mess it created.

Industry defenders embraced a more pragmatic argument as well. They insisted that the social and economic costs of a government S & L rescue would be significantly lower than the costs associated with liquidation. The collapse of the industry could, they continued, undermine public confidence in all financial institutions, resulting in exorbitant economic and social costs. To bolster their argument, industry spokesmen added that the actual, estimated cost of a government bail-out would be considerably less than that incurred following a closure of even one-third of the nation's S & Ls.[15]

So, which side was telling the truth? An objective assessment of the situation suggests that neither side was completely correct, or balanced, in its assertion. Despite the cries of capitalist purists, government had for many years prior to the S & L crisis interfered in the operations of these institutions. On the other hand, blaming government—specifically, the Fed—was not totally fair either, as many of the Board's actions seemed at the time perfectly prudent; and, of course, the consequences of a tight-money policy were hardly limited to S & Ls.

Beyond philosophy and ideology, one important fact made an S & L rescue by the federal government inevitable: nationwide, about 5,000 thrifts were in operation, with at least a few in each of the 435 congressional districts.[16] The industry, recognizing the likely political consequences of government inaction, behaved accordingly; that is, it demanded attention. In so demanding, however, industry leaders had to consider carefully the all-important question: What was required for recovery?

Devising an approach to saving the thrift industry was a joint effort, with ongoing input from government officials and industry leaders. In the following section we examine the legislative and regulatory steps finally taken by government to implement this rescue.

THE GOVERNMENT IN REACTION

The main problems facing U.S. S & Ls in the 1979–82 period involved earnings and liquidity. In the long run, earnings reflect an institution's viability, but in the short run it is liquidity that counts most.[17] In responding to the industry's crisis, the national government took steps to alleviate difficulties associated with each of these measures of S & L health. It was, in effect, attempting to liberate S & Ls.

Among the many federal policies designed to free thrifts was the critically important package of amendments to the Housing and Community Development Act. These amendments, passed in 1979, once again increased the ceiling on single-family loan limits for association lending, federal agency purchases, and FHA insurance. One of the amendments included an exemption from state usury laws for all FHA loans. Such laws, in this case set by each state individually, place legal limits on the maximum interest that can be charged on a particular type of loan.

Another major regulatory change, approved by the FHLBB in 1979, granted the authority to federally chartered S & Ls to offer variable-rate mortgages (VRMs), graduated-payment mortgages, and reverse-annuity mortgages.[18] Initially, the controversial VRMs were restricted to those institutions operating in states where state-chartered thrifts were permitted to offer them, but beginning July 1, 1979, the FHLBB extended such authority to all federal associations.[19]

In April of the same year both Congress and the U.S. judiciary got into the act, when the Court of Appeals for the District of Columbia called upon the national legislature to act, one way or the other, in deciding whether certain S & L practices would theretofore be permissible. The court had ruled that various regulatory bodies had exceeded their legal authority by allowing banks to use Automatic Transfer Accounts (ATs), allowing credit unions to issue drafts, and allowing S & Ls to use remote service units. Such practices, the court held, unless validated by Congress, would have to cease by January 1, 1980. Thus Congress was forced to act. As congressional leaders began grappling with these regulatory matters, they viewed the opportunity as one to act on other reforms as well.

The result was a comprehensive piece of legislation, one that the Senate and the House of Representatives haggled over incessantly. The most important disagreement between the two houses was over the controversial Regulation Q. In addition, legislators quarreled over authorization for NOW accounts and various proposals involving membership in the Fed.

As the congressional debate heightened in intensity and detail, it became evident that more time was needed to resolve differences, particularly over the issue of phasing out Regulation Q. In order to avoid missing the court-ordered deadline, both houses agreed to a 90-day extension of the deadline. During the extension the House, in considering the phase-out issue, began to soften. Eventually, compromise was reached on every major reform proposal. The final bill, drafted as the Depository Institutions Deregulation and Monetary Control Act, was signed into law by President Jimmy Carter on March 31, 1980—the final day of the extension.[20]

The key feature of the DIDMCA was a six-year phase-out of deposit-rate ceilings, but several other provisions directly impacted S & Ls, including ones permitting these institutions to offer NOW accounts; trust services; and mutual capital certificates;[21] engage in credit card activities; invest up to 20 percent of assets in consumer loans; provide commercial paper and corporate debt securities; and make first or second mortgage loans without regard to size or geographic restrictions. Another important feature of the law was a raise in the limit on S & L investment in service corporations, from 1 to 3 percent of total assets.[22] Congress also assisted thrifts via the FHLBB, by authorizing the agency to lower the federal insurance reserve requirement from 5 to 3 percent of the deposit base. In addition, S & L officials were delighted by the increase in individual-account deposit insurance from $40,000 to $100,000, and the preemption of all state mortgage usury laws (subject to the right of a state to reinstate such laws within three years). Finally, Congress, which at one time opposed VRMs, left the issue of these mortgages to be decided by federal regulations.[23]

The critical shift on Regulation Q ceilings left many industry observers wondering: Why did it take Congress such time and labor to terminate them? In fact, Congress had two good reasons for making the shift slowly. First, many experts believed that the ceilings kept the cost of funds to S & Ls lower than what they likely would have been. Consequently, this meant that thrifts could charge less for mortgages than would have been possible without the ceilings.[24] Second, supporters of ceilings believed that S & Ls' financial problems, in the absence of ceilings, would have worsened during times of disintermediation.[25] Thus Congress, though appearing slow and indecisive, actually behaved, in this instance, quite prudently.

Passage of the DIDMCA left many observers baffled, particularly in view of the fact that so many less grandiose efforts at reform, such as the FIA, had failed. However, a careful examination of events and trends suggests why, by 1980, the time for reform had arrived. Indeed, Kenneth McLean, staff director of the Senate Committee on Banking, Housing and Urban Affairs in 1980, offered four reasons why DIDMCA passed. First, rising inflation and the corresponding high market interest rates during the late 1970s and 1980 had worked to penalize savers, thus discouraging them from relying on accounts in depository institutions; this, in turn, greatly reduced the level of funds available for capital expenditures. Second, deregulation efforts in other sectors of the national economy were generally viewed as successful; this alleviated the fears of many legislators about the consequences of deregulating S & Ls. Third, by 1979 money market mutual funds were well established and had effectively eliminated the impact of interest-rate ceilings on all but the smallest and most conservative savers. Finally, McLean argued, the American Bankers Association had switched sides in the debate over NOW accounts; by 1980 it was, in fact, actively supporting them.[26]

Financial analysts disagree about the overall impact of the DIDMCA's passage. While some hail it as the most significant legislative development in financial institutions' affairs since the 1930s,[27] others contend that, far from being a move toward deregulation, it represented even *more* regulation.[28] Whether it was good or bad, regulatory or deregulatory, the DIDMCA's passage—which *mandated* certain specific S & L changes, and *permitted* others—clearly altered the character of the U.S. thrift industry.

As important as the DIDMCA was, however, not even its staunchest supporters expected it to deliver miracles. Indeed, by the time of its passage, the nation was experiencing economic and financial dilemmas that were not about to disappear overnight, or on account of any single new law. Most significantly, by late 1980 rising interest rates were taking a heavy toll on the S & L industry. While nationally S & Ls reported a collective profit of $800 million for 1980, over 30 percent of all institutions reported second-half losses. In the first six months of 1981, the industry recorded its first semiannual loss since the creation of the FHLBB. That loss ($1.5 billion) was, however, more than doubled in the second half of that year, climbing to $3.1 billion.

While many particular problems contributed to the industry's worsening condition, most troubling to S & L officials was how widespread the difficulties had become. That is, in the second half of 1980 85 percent of U.S. S & Ls actually reported losses.[29] Moreover, the problem of disintermediation—less-publicized than losses per se, but of no less long-term importance—was threatening the stability of S & Ls from coast to coast. This condition, commonly referred to as a "silent run," portended disaster as, by 1981, the combined losses of insured associations in net new savings exceeded $25 billion.[30]

In response to the outflow of thrift deposits the industry introduced new financial instruments, designed to attract new deposits with profit potential. First, in 1980, a Small-Savers certificate was authorized. Similar to the six-month money market certificate, it nevertheless provides a yield keyed to that on 30-month Treasury certificates. It further stands apart from the MMC in that it has a 30-month maturity and no minimum denomination.[31]

Another step toward competitiveness in the deposits market came in March 1982, when the Depository Institutions Deregulation Committee (DIDC) authorized creation of the 91-day certificate of deposit. Here the maximum yield would equal that on 13-week Treasury Bills issued by thrift institutions and mutual savings banks, while commercial banks were restricted to a yield rate .25 percent lower. This 91-day certificate differed from the six-month MMC in that the former would require a minimum deposit of $7,500 instead of $10,000.[32]

In June 1982 the DIDC again assisted thrifts by approving a $20,000 minimum daily balance account, with a maximum yield pegged to the three-month Treasury Bill yield for S & Ls (.25 percent above that of banks' yields). Maturity on the account could range from 7 to 31 days. The first of these accounts could be opened September 1, 1982.[33]

Along with the 91-day account the DIDC declared that, beginning May 1, 1982, the ceiling on *all* accounts maturing in three and one-half years or more would be effectively eliminated. Because this seemed to give thrifts too great an advantage over banks, the DIDC decided that the aforementioned differential favoring thrifts would last one year only, and would not apply when the Treasury Bill rate fell below 9 percent.[34]

The federal government further aided the S & L industry, in two important ways, via its 1981 Economic Recovery Act. First, the law provided for the creation of an All-Savers Certificate. With a one-year maturity, this certificate would give the saver a rate up to 70 percent of the yield on comparable one-year Treasury securities. More importantly, the interest income would be tax-exempt, provided that, on a lifetime basis, it did not exceed $1,000 per person. Second, the universal IRA was permitted. Previously IRAs had been restricted to workers who did not contribute to a pension fund in a given year. Under the new law, IRAs became available to all workers.[35]

Congress went further in enhancing the competitive posture of thrifts by passing the Garn–St. Germain Depository Institutions Act. Effective in 1982, this law reshaped the practices of the nation's thrifts. First, it authorized the FHLBB to make loans to, deposits in, or purchases of assets of any thrift institution, provided the action was taken to prevent the thrift's default, or to restore its normal operation.[36] (While this was an important step symbolically, it meant little in concrete practice, as the Board had for over two years already been engaging in such activities; thus it merely legitimized such practices.)

A second feature of Garn–St. Germain, one with vast potential for troubled thrifts, authorized Net Worth Certificates.[37] This fresh approach to assisting S & Ls allowed the FHLBB to purchase equity in the institutions themselves. A limit to the Board's purchases was established, one based on operating losses and the extent to which the institution's net worth had eroded.[38]

However, in deference to market laws, the act provided that in no instance would the Board be authorized to expend a sum greater than the cost of liquidation.[39]

Garn–St. Germain also provided new guidelines for S & L mergers and acquisitions. This key provision was intended to restore to the industry some semblance of order, as it had, in the few months preceding the law's passage, been jolted by frenzied merger activity. These guidelines affected merger candidates of all types: institutions of the same type within the same state, of the same type in different states, of different types in the same state, and of different types in different states.[40] Basically, the guidelines discouraged mergers that seemed detrimental to the industry's long-term well-being.

In a final move, designed to diversify the asset structure of the thrift industry, investment authority was granted, along the following lines:

1. Nonresidential real estate loans: an increase in the maximum lending authority, from 20 to 40 percent of assets;

2. Consumer loans: an increase in the maximum lending authority, from 20 to 30 percent of assets;

3. Commercial loans: permitting up to 10 percent of assets to be invested in loans for commercial or business purposes; and

4. State securities: permitting thrift institutions to invest without limit in tax-exempt banks.[41]

Among these provisions, the most significant involved commercial lending, where authority theretofore had rested, almost entirely in the hands of commercial banks and, in a few of the states (Texas included), in state-chartered S & Ls.

In a move designed to improve the industry's liquidity, the DIA authorized two new liability accounts. One, the money market deposit account, was authorized for banks and S & Ls. It would feature no minimum maturity and no control over interest rates. Finally, although no reserve requirement existed, it provided for limited transactions. The other was a Corporate and Business Transaction Account, established to complement the newly acquired commercial lending authority of S & Ls.[42]

Perhaps the most important step taken by the DIA was the preemption of various "due-on-sale" laws existing in many states. Prior to this time, when a homeowner in one of these states sold a home, any outstanding mortgage could be assumed by the buyer. Frequently these mortgages were of the older, low-yield variety—the type that in the 1970s and early 1980s had caused S & Ls so many problems. The new provisions, however, empowered thrifts to call a mortgage due and payable upon sale of the house.[43] From a practical standpoint this meant that S & Ls would be able to renegotiate the mortgage at the current market rate. Naturally this delighted S & L officials, as it permitted associations to upgrade their mortgage portfolio without ever having to record losses.

OTHER S & L PROBLEMS

Despite the boost given them via federal deregulation in the early 1980s, thrifts faced a variety of difficulties untouched by such legislation. In many cases such problems threatened bankruptcy; in others, they meant ongoing operating losses. These problems centered, almost without exception, around interest rates.

By 1980 the interest-rate yield curve was inverted (that is, short-term rates exceeded long-term rates). This condition created severe financial difficulties for thrifts, which were forced to pay high rates to acquire funds, while receiving relatively low returns from mortgage loans made in previous years. Consequently, many institutions found themselves on the brink of insolvency.

Troubled S & Ls needed immediate help in the form of income, and they had two choices available to them. The first was failure (or acquisition, which in cases of financially burdened thrifts is tantamount to failure). The second choice was to engage in high-risk, fast-income projects. The most popular such project involved charging points[44] at the origination of a loan.

A handy way for S & Ls to earn points (i.e., quick income) was through acquisition, development, and construction (ADC) loans. Such loans became popular in the early 1980s because they allowed thrifts to share in the earnings of joint ventures with investment developers. In such cases the S & L would make the loan for a total development project, including purchase of the property, the cost of interim construction, and any additional costs (e.g., interest, points, etc.). Such loans are attractive to investors, as they tie into a single, convenient loan all financial obligations, with the S & L providing 100 percent financing. This meant, of course, that S & Ls bear 100 percent of the risk, also. The institutions tend to be equally enthusiastic about such ventures, mostly because they are able to charge investors additional points on the loans.[45]

In the early 1980s points on S & L ADC loans were counted as income at the time of loan origination. Ideally, these loans would be paid off at the completion of various development projects (e.g., shopping malls), and their subsequent sale. Because the projects were fully financed by thrifts, they, along with the developers, would reap handsome profits.[46] So for the S & L industry this scheme promised quick income—which most S & Ls sorely needed.

One major problem associated with ADC loans was the difficulty S & Ls encountered when attempting to obtain funds sufficient to meet project costs. With interest rates in excess of 10 percent, thrifts needed to offer higher rates in order to lure depositors away from money market funds. The solution came in the form of "brokered funds": large amounts of money pooled by investors seeking maximum return on their investments.

Thus an S & L in need of cash approached brokers, offering interest rates above the rates offered in other financial markets. In the process, many such loans were secured.[47] While this resulted in a great many profitable sales of completed projects, other ADC projects never were sold, or were sold at a loss. In either of these cases, the institution's financial posture was worsened: it suffered either a direct loss or the addition to its books of a non-income-earning asset, at a time when the institution's income, as evidenced by its willingness to engage in such high-risk activity, was low in the first place. Why did this occur so often? Because, unlike with most projects, "investors" in ADC-funded projects had little or no financial stake in the project, and thus had disincentive to follow through on these deals.

Through various ways and means, U.S. S & Ls struggled to cope with the industry's crisis of the early 1980s. While many succeeded, a great number of others could not successfully compete, and were forced either to close or to merge with stronger institutions. Had it not been for the decline in interest rates realized in late 1982, many more S & Ls would almost certainly have disappeared.

TEXAS S & Ls: 1979–82

While most U.S. thrift institutions were reeling in the early 1980s, state-chartered S & Ls in Texas were sailing along nicely. Not only did most institutions escape the industry's crisis unscathed, many of them enjoyed continuous growth throughout. Indeed, at the beginning of 1979 the assets of Texas thrifts totaled $27.8 billion, and by the end of 1982 the figure had grown to more than $42 billion—an increase of 50 percent during a time when, all across the United States, other thrifts were scrambling for mere survival. What accounted for Texas' success? The answer lies, to a great extent, in the makeup of the state's economy.

During the 1960s and 1970s, when the "Sunbelt" region of the country experienced such huge increases in population, income, housing, and commerce, Texas enjoyed broad, general prosperity. At the same time, the state's oil industry, owing primarily to the Organization of Petroleum Exporting Countries' (OPEC) doubling of crude oil prices, prospered like never before. As a result, oil-related interests in Texas—which are many—thrived as well. Together, these developments necessarily aided those industries, thrifts included, that rely on economic expansion for growth.

In fact, the state's S & Ls had a difficult time keeping up with demands for loans, as the need for drilling equipment, pipelines, storage tanks, oil trucks, and other items continued to increase. Besides this demand for industrial materials, there was a simultaneous demand for new office buildings, and for homes and apartment complexes to house the expected influx of new workers. Thus beyond the oil industry itself there appeared a great demand for secondary service workers to support new industry. Along with this pickup in the state's economy, S & L officials believed, should come a revamped approach to thrift practices. Hence, they proceeded to call for new legislation designed to facilitate Texas' overall growth by liberalizing S & L practices. The following section offers an examination of the significant rules and regulations passed in response to industry pressure on state lawmakers and regulators.

REGULATORY PROVISIONS FOR GROWTH IN THE TEXAS S & L INDUSTRY

The first important change in rules governing Texas state-chartered thrifts occurred in July 1979 with the creation of a longer term mortgage. This change, designed to enhance consumer borrowing, permitted a loan term with a maximum of 40 years, up from a maximum of 30 years.[48] Consequently, buyers had the option of securing home loans with lower monthly payments.

In that same year the Texas Finance Commission approved a variable interest-rate loan. This loan provided the consumer another option in home financing, in addition to the standard, fixed-rate loan. This eased the fears of potential borrowers concerned about financing during periods of high fixed rates. That is, with fixed-rate loans, buyers are locked into high payment schemes even during years of low interest rates; this way, when interest rates fall generally, mortgage payments fall along with them.

A third means enabling Texas thrifts to increase their loan volume involved the creation of graduated-payment loans. Under this scheme new home buyers may begin paying their mortgages with relatively low monthly installments, and increase payments as their incomes increase.[49]

Two years later, in 1981, Texas thrifts were assisted by a regulatory shift making it easier for individual associations to open branch offices. Prior to this time the guidelines for opening new offices had a very restrictive feature. The key to the restriction contained in the law was that only one branch at a time could be established by any S & L. On March 31, 1981, the regulation was changed to read as follows:

Each application for permission to establish a branch office shall state the proposed location thereof; the need thereof; the personnel and office facilities to be provided; the estimated accrual volume of business, income and expense of such office and shall be accompanied by a proposed annual budget of the applying association. Each application for a branch office shall be set for hearing, notice given, hearing held, and decision reached in the same manner and within the time as herein provided for new charter applications and the hearing may be dispensed with under the same conditions.[50]

Thus the amended regulation provided thrifts the freedom to apply for more than one branch at a time. Moreover, they would be able to apply for additional branches while the commission deliberated on previous branch applications. This regulatory change represented a major victory for the state's S & L industry.

Also in 1981 the Finance Commission granted state-chartered thrifts permission to use remote unit services. Such services were sure to attract many new customers to S & Ls, as they made transactions much simpler and more convenient. In addition, the introduction of this practice at thrifts made it possible for them to compete effectively with commercial banks for individual deposits. Again, the commission's rule change was simple and direct:

Remote Service Unit means an information processing device, to be operated off premises of an approved savings and loan office, includings associated equipment structures and systems, by which information relating to financial services rendered the public is stored and transmitted simultaneously or otherwise to a financial institution. The term includes any facility which for activation and account access requires the use of an activator and personal identifier in the possession of the user and includes "on line" computer terminals, and "on line" cases dispersing machines and automated teller machines. A remote service is not an office of the association within the meaning of Section 2.13 of the "Texas Savings and Loan Act."[51]

One of the most revolutionary changes in Texas S & L governance was one involving the percentage of project financing permitted associations. Prior to October 1981, the most an S & L could lend was 95 percent of the appraised value, or purchase price, of a given project. But thereafter thrifts would be permitted to finance 100 percent of a project. Although this presented a degree of increased risk for S & Ls, their leaders wholeheartedly endorsed the change.

As written, the law provided that a loan could be made based on appraised value or purchase price—the lesser of the two:

Every association may make or purchase participations in real estate loans secured by a mortgage, deed of trust, or other instrument creating or constituting a first and proper lien on real estate in the amount of 100% of the appraised value or the purchase price, *whichever is less*, of said property. Provided further, such real estate loans must be within the same terms and limits specified. . . . [52]

However, this did not prevent Texas S & Ls from making loans based on the *greater* of the two values, and in many cases this occurred. This is because, although the specific state provisions called for loans limited to the lesser value, all state S & Ls enjoyed added flexibility in their practices, as the state code made clear: "Every association may make or participate in any kind, type or character of loan authorized or approved for a federal association doing business in this state."[53] In 1981 Congress passed a law similar to the state's *Rules and Regulations*, section 8.1 (B), permitting 100 percent financing, but also allowing financing of the greater amount (appraised value or purchase price). Hence Texas State-chartered thrifts had absolute freedom in determining loan amounts for these projects.

This freedom, welcomed by affected S & Ls across the country as well as those in Texas, brought with it considerable risk. For national thrifts, it is viewed by many experts as the biggest mistake made by the FHLBB in recent years.[54] This is because many investors who received inflated appraisals were eligible for loans equal to those appraisals, and in many cases the additional capital was used for other projects. Then, if and when real estate values declined—as occurred frequently in the early-

and mid-1980s—investors would default on their loans. So the S & Ls were often stuck with non-income-producing real estate, now valued at *much* less than the amounts originally loaned. This resulted in enormous decreases in the net worth of affected S & Ls; for accounting purposes, such loans would be taken off the books and replaced by assets of lower value, carried in non-income-earning accounts called "Real Estate Owned."[55]

For S & Ls with federal charters, this option created many problems during the years of real estate decline. As will be shown, a number of Texas state-chartered thrifts found themselves in trouble after utilizing this risky option, especially when the loans were based on misleading income statements and balance sheets, which led to greatly inflated appraisals.[56]

Two additional rules, passed in 1981, further served to enhance S & L growth and satisfy consumer demands. They involved Negotiable Orders of Withdrawal and checking accounts, and were established as follows:

Any association may, when authorized by its Board of Directors, permit the withdrawal of funds from savings accounts by means of negotiable orders of withdrawal payable to third parties, provided all documentation meets applicable statutory and regulatory requirements.[57]

And, directly following:

Any deposit type association whose bylaws contain the priority provisions authorized by Section 6.19 of the "Texas Savings and Loan Act," may, when authorized by its Board of Directors, permit the withdrawal of funds from deposit accounts (interest-bearing or not) by means of checks to the order to third parties drawn by the account holder and payable by the association upon presentation in accordance with the uniform commercial code of the state.[58]

Together, these rule changes provided consumers with new, attractive services and resulted in substantially higher deposits in the state's S & Ls.

Another means by which the consumer was satisfied involved overdraft protection. Formerly, no such protection was permitted, but on March 31, 1981, the S & L code was amended to read as follows:

An association which permits withdrawals from accounts in the manner authorized by 9.10, 9.11 and 9.12 of this chapter, may offer in connection with such accounts overdraft protection to account holders in the form of revolving loans and may offer revolving tri-party arrangements (credit and debit cards) under Chapter 15 of the "Texas Credit Code" provided the total net amount advanced at any time to any one account shall not exceed $10,000.[59]

When the Texas Finance Commission approved this amendment, it hoped to assist state thrifts in attracting new customers. To this extent, the commission clearly succeeded.

While all of these rules worked to stimulate growth among Texas state-chartered S & Ls, they brought with them some problems as well. In the following section we examine the plight of one institution that, in the process of stunning growth, suffered a fate so dismal that it drew national attention to the state's thrift industry.[60]

TOO MUCH, TOO SOON: THE CASE OF EMPIRE S & L

Among the many Texas S & Ls that grew very rapidly in the early 1980s was the Empire S & L Association of Mesquite, Texas. However, by 1984 FHLBB Chairman Edwin Gray openly characterized the Empire situation as "a gigantic fraud" and said that it "represents one of the most reckless and fraudulent land investment schemes we have ever encountered at this agency. It was characterized by self-dealing and sheer greed."[61]

Empire's problems first came to the attention of the FHLBB on October 7, 1982. During the Board's regular supervisory examination of the S & L it found "significant examination factors" rated as either material deficiencies or requiring immediate forceful supervision action.[62] Still, another year passed before the FHLBB took action.

A major problem for Empire was that most of its "loans" for real estate acquisition and development were, for all practical purposes, *investments*. Hence, borrowers were taking few risks, while Empire bore the risks of an equity participant and loan provider. At the same time, Empire was charging points on these loans, and treating the income derived therefrom as up-front capital, even though such income (if it came from a true investment) normally would be counted only when the given property were sold, or otherwise relinquished. (This particular practice, it should be noted, was common among S & Ls throughout the nation. It was, in the case of Empire, just one of many practices that led to disaster.)[63]

Before Empire reached the point of insolvency it experienced incredible growth. In mid-1982 its assets totaled only $17.3 million; less than two years later the figure had swollen to $309 million. By this time, however, the association had been struggling with imposing problems for a year. Indeed, by the time Empire reached its asset peak, it was already doomed; on March 14, 1984, the FHLBB, having determined that Empire's unprecedented growth was primarily the result of numerous, risky real estate acquisitions and development loans, closed the S & L's doors.[64]

Had the FHLBB paid close attention sooner, it would have recognized Empire's unsound footing, the result of dangerous industry practices. For example, the Southwest S & L industry's average ratio of nonindustrial mortgage loans to total loans was 12 percent; but by the end of 1982 Empire had a ratio of 48 percent. Furthermore, while the percentage growth of total loans, industry-wide, was 7 percent in 1982, Empire's growth during that year was 137 percent.[65]

Empire's irregular practices showed up in many other categories as well. Indeed, in 1982 the industry-wide loan yield was 11 percent, while Empire's was 21 percent. The ratio of Jumbo Certificates of Deposit to earning assets was 6 percent for the industry but an astonishing 64 percent for Empire. (Significantly, when Empire was shut down, $262 million, or 85 percent of its $309 million in deposits was in the form of brokered funds.)[66]

Upon request by the FHLBB, Cates Consulting Analysts examined Empire's books and presented the Board with its findings, which began: "The Empire financial performance of 1982 appeared to us so wildly irregular—and so reminiscent of pre-failure performance at Penn Square, Midland, Abilene, etc.—that I promptly dubbed Empire 'the Penn Square of the thrift industry.' "[67]

Further examination revealed that Empire's chairman of the board, Spencer H. Blain, was involved in various illegal activities. One such activity involved the purchase of 65.92 acres of land in August 1982, for $986,000. Six months later the land was sold—for $16 million. The buyer, it turns out, was a major customer of Empire. The FHLBB deemed this, of course, a conflict of interest and a usurpation of corporate authority.[68]

On other occasions Empire was involved in so-called land flips, two of which occurred in late 1982. First, on October 8, 6.6 acres of land were sold to KB and P, Inc., for $392,113, or $1.35 per square foot. On that same day, KB and P sold the land to Cascade Properties for $1,379,469, or $4.75 per square foot. The purchase was made possible by a loan, from Empire, of $1,414,531, or $4.87 per square foot. Then on November 18, Kiteo Developers sold 3.6 acres of land for $156,816, or $1.00 per square foot. On the same day, the land was resold to Bob Ward Enterprises, Inc., for $1,332,936, or $8.50 per square foot, with Empire making the latter a loan of $1,525,257, or $9.73 per square foot.[69] Because of these "flips," land prices were artificially inflated, and the loans on such projects were far in excess of market value.[70]

The aforementioned practices led to, among other things, an overbuilding of condominiums, especially on the I-30 corridor east of Dallas. This was caused by an abundance of land and construction loans for the area's development, leading to excessive building. A great many of these loans were made by Empire.[71]

By January 9, 1984, the FHLBB was ready to move, and did so by calling for a "cease and desist" order, effectively crippling Empire. On the same day, the Texas S & L Department took voluntary control of Empire. The institution was ultimately closed on March 14, 1984.[72]

To industry analysts the questions that arose from the Empire situation were simple. First, how did it ever happen? Second, inasmuch as the problems and irregularities were discovered two years before the thrift's closure, why did it take so long? The answers to these questions were provided during the Subcommittee Hearing on the adequacy of the FHLBB supervision of Empire, on April 25, 1984. At this time the Board offered the following explanation:

At the present time, the Bank Board lacks authority to take swift and effective action when our examiners discover that an institution's books and records are seriously incomplete or in disarray. Bank Board regulations presently require the maintenance of accurate books and records, so the Agency may issue a Notice of Charges alleging such a violation and proceed to litigate the matter in an APA hearing (which typically consumes a minimum of 9 months to complete). But the existing statutory grounds for issuance of a temporary C&D order are so strict that they cannot be employed unless the Board can make a finding that the violation or unsafe or unsound practice in question is likely to cause insolvency or dissipation of assets of earning or is likely to seriously weaken the financial condition of the institution. Clearly, this is an exceedingly difficult level of proof absent a thorough review of the books and records which first must be reconstructed.[73]

So it was, because of the Empire case, that the Texas S & L Code for 1985 contained major revisions in the area of supervisory control. Under the new code the state S & L Commission was given greater "cease and desist" authority.[74]

TEXAS S & Ls, 1979–82: FEDERAL VERSUS STATE

Despite the fact that the Texas S & L industry grew in asset size during the 1979–82 period, several individual S & Ls did not survive the crisis that marked those years. The combination of an inverted yield curve and low-interest mortgages held by the S & Ls was, in many cases, too burdensome for these institutions, and they simply collapsed.

During these years one of the most noticeable trends in the Texas S & L industry was the drop in the number of mutual institutions, from 34 state-chartered mutuals to 22, and, among mutuals with federal charters, a decrease of 19, from 68 to 49.[75]

Such declines should not be surprising when one considers that, during this crisis era, most thrifts were struggling just to maintain a positive net worth. For stocks S & Ls the task was somewhat easier, as they had the option of selling stock to raise capital. But with mutuals no such option was available and, as net worth diminished, many of these S & Ls became insolvent, while many others sought mergers.

Still, even the number of stock S & Ls in Texas declined over this time—from 221 to 209 (over the same period Texas-based federal stock associations grew in number, from one to four).[76] Overall, however, stock associations outperformed their mutual counterparts during this very difficult era, and the main advantage they enjoyed was the ability to raise capital from outside sources.

In terms of accumulated assets during the 1979–82 period, state-chartered thrifts easily outshone those S & Ls with federal charters. In 1979 state S & Ls boasted combined assets of $23.8 billion, and by 1982 the figure had risen to $35.6 billion. But the comparable totals for Texas associations with federal charters were $7.7 billion and $7.8 billion.[77] (These two figures are somewhat misleading, however, as the number of federally chartered thrifts decreased; the remaining ones, while generally lagging behind state-chartered S & Ls, nevertheless fared pretty well.)

The figures representing the net worth of Texas S & Ls during this three-year span are not good, either for federal or state institutions. Over this period federally chartered thrifts suffered an aggregate drop in net worth from $448 million to $308 million. State-chartered S & Ls did somewhat better, as they saw their combined net worth grow from $1.18 billion in 1979 to $1.29 billion in 1982.[78]

The main factor accounting for the decline in net worth among Texas' federally chartered S & Ls was, again, that most of them featured mutual ownership and consequently had difficulty raising needed capital. Conversely, Texas state-chartered thrifts fared well during this time largely because the great majority of them were of the stock variety.

Another area in which state-chartered S & Ls outperformed federal institutions in Texas was that of nontraditional loans (e.g., commercial loans and consumer loans). Indeed, it was discovered that the return on these loans—dominated by state-chartered S & Ls, particularly those featuring stock ownership—was greater than that on standard mortgage loans.[79] In a study, prepared for the FHLBB by John Crockett and A. Thomas King, the authors further pointed out that

> the average annual return (on the basis of semiannual flows) over the period was forty basis points for the state stocks, thirty-five basis points for the state mutuals and thirty-three basis points for the federal mutuals. These results indicate that there are observable differences in the average performance of the three groups. Note that the biggest difference is between the state stocks and mutuals. This is consistent with a variety of the other evidence suggesting that stock S & Ls are more aggressive and profit-oriented than mutuals are.[80]

Crockett and King's findings suggest that the success of state-chartered institutions in Texas, relative to federal S & Ls, was due largely to the high percentage of the latter possessing mutual charters. Many observers have offered another view, noting that during the 1979–82 crisis, state-chartered S & Ls experienced little success. They point out that during these three years state-chartered mutual thrifts declined in number by 35 percent, while federally chartered mutuals decreased by only 28 percent. Finally, Dr. Jack Cashin, former executive vice president of the Texas S & L League, takes still another position. He argues: "It was not so much what type of charter the Texas S & L had, but how careful they were in making their loans that made the difference in how well the association fared during the early 1980s."[81]

SUMMARY: 1979–82

The three-year period 1979–82 was a difficult one for the entire S & L industry. Each of these years saw hundreds of institutions close, mostly because the cost of securing funds was so high, and the returns on their long-standing mortgages were too low. Nevertheless, despite the predictions of many experts during this crisis, the industry itself did not buckle under. What occurred instead was a wave of innovation, both in asset accounts and liability accounts of S & Ls. New means of securing funds through such instruments as Small Savers Certificates,

91-day certificates, and money market deposit accounts helped the industry avert disaster that a liquidity crisis could have caused.

New loan types, such as ARMS (Adjustable Rate Mortgages), helped S & Ls decrease risks associated with interest rates. Other, more profitable short-term loans were permitted for commercial and consumer loans, attracting many new customers in the process.

In general, the industry's survival seems to have been made possible by its leaders' willingness, and ability, to undergo change. For Texas S & Ls the period was one of growth coupled with radical changes in lending practices. As we have seen, high oil prices combined with a series of new regulations facilitated rapid industry growth throughout the state. However as we shall see in Chapter 6, this growth may have been excessive, as the post-1982 era would feature severe S & L problems for Texas as well as the entire nation.

NOTES

1. "A Real Inflation Fighter Takes Charge at the Fed," *Fortune,* September 10, 1979, p. 62.

2. The prime rate is the interest rate that commercial banks charge on loans to their most creditworthy customers. The prime rate is a good barometer for other interest rates because most other rates follow the movements, up or down, of the prime rate.

3. The prime interest rate reached a monthly average peak of 20.50 percent in August 1981.

4. A yield curve shows the relationship between interest yields and term to maturity. A "normal" yield curve will shape upward, which means that a higher interest rate will be paid on longer-term securities.

5. Loan origination fees generally average 1 to 2 percent of the value of the loan. During the early 1980s such fees ran as high as 10 to 12 percent of the loan value. These excessive fees were charged by several Texas S & Ls on their acquisition, development, and construction loans.

6. Eugene Guyon, "A Critical Review of the Savings and Loan Industry," Professional Report, The University of Texas, Austin, 1983, p. 16. Money market mutual funds are those invested by individuals

whose primary objective is to make higher interest securities available to investors who want quick income and high investment safety.

7. Asset portfolio yield is the return received by a firm (S & L) on the assets held by the firm.

8. A secondary market is one where loans can be sold if the S & L no longer wishes to hold a certain loan. Fannie Mae and Freddie Mac are secondary markets for mortgage loans made by S & Ls.

9. Rickard Kupcke, "The Condition of Massachusetts Savings Banks and California Savings and Loan Associations," in *The Future of the Thrift Industry* (Boston: Federal Reserve Bank of Boston, 1981), p. 4. During the early 1980s many S & Ls were securing a large percentage of their funds through borrowings from commercial banks and from Federal Home Loan Bank advances.

10. Return on equity is found by dividing net after-tax income by average net worth. Return on average assets is found by dividing net after-tax income by average assets.

11. Guyon, p. 18.

12. "The Future Role of Thrift Institutions in Mortgage Lending," Proceedings of a conference on the Future of the Thrift Industry, October 1981 (Boston: Federal Reserve Bank of Boston, 1981), p. 168.

13. *Ibid.*, p. 44.

14. *Ibid.*

15. Guyon, p. 20.

16. "S & Ls Show Their Political Punch," *Business Week*, November 23, 1981, p. 114.

17. Earnings basically come from a company's income. Liquidity basically refers to the ability to convert an asset into cash without significant loss.

18. A variable-rate mortgage is one that allows payments to adjust upward or downward following some market interest rate. Graduated-payment mortgages allow the payments to increase, at some set rate, over the life of a loan. A reverse-annuity mortgage is one in which the borrower pledges real estate as collateral, but then the lender provides monthly payments to the borrower. When the mortgage matures, the borrower owes one lump-sum payment.

19. Indeed, the desire to authorize VRMs was not a new one. Recently, each one of the 1970s FHLBB chairmen has indicated that, among his regrets as board chairman, was his inability to implement VRM authority. William K. Divers, Statement, *Federal Home Loan Bank Board Journal*, April 1982, pp. 81–88.

20. Walter J. Woerheide, *The Savings and Loan Industry: Current Problems and Possible Solutions* (Westport, Conn.: Quorum Books, 1984), p. 19.

21. Mutual Capital Certificates are a form of subordinated debt in a mutual corporation. These certificates are issued in order to give mutual S & Ls a means of obtaining net worth from sources outside of the institution.

22. Although S & Ls investments in service corporations increased from 1 to 3 percent of total assets, one-half of the increase had to go to the financing of low- and middle-income housing.

23. U.S. Congress, *The Depository Institutions Deregulatory and Monetary Control Act of 1980*, sec. 202(d).

24. Ken McLean, "Legislative Background of the Depository Institutions Deregulation and Monetary Control Act of 1980," *Savings and Loan Asset Management Under Deregulation: Proceedings of the Sixth Annual Conference*, Federal Home Loan Bank of San Francisco, 1980, p. 23.

25. *Ibid.*

26. Woerheide, p. 20.

27. Robert C. West, "The Depository Institutions Deregulation Act of 1980: A Historical Perspective," *Economic Review*, Federal Reserve Bank of Kansas City, February 1982, p. 3.

28. Edward Kane, "Deregulation, Savings and Loan Diversification and the Flow of Housing Finance," *Savings and Loan Asset Management Under Deregulation: Proceedings of the Sixth Annual Conference*, Federal Home Loan Bank of San Francisco, 1980.

29. Timothy D. Scheldhardt, "S & Ls Had Recorded 4.6 Billion Loss in 1981; $6 Billion Deficit Seen Possible This Year," *Wall Street Journal*, April 6, 1982.

30. *1982 Savings and Loan Source Book* (Chicago: United States League of Savings Institutions, 1983), p. 21.

31. The standard practice of most S & Ls was to impose a $100 minimum denomination on these small saver's certificates.

32. "Banks, Thrifts Can Offer, Starting May 1, 91-Day Certificates Paying Market Rates," *Wall Street Journal*, March 23, 1982, p. 2.

33. "Savings Accord to Help Banks, S & Ls is Cleared," *Wall Street Journal*, June 30, 1982.

34. *Ibid.*

35. Woerheide, p. 22.

36. Guyon, p. 43.

37. Net worth certificates were issued and bought by the FHLBB to increase the capital position of failing S & Ls.

38. *Depository Institutions Act*, sec. 202(a).

39. *Ibid.*

40. *Ibid.*, sec. 116.

41. *Ibid.*, sec. 321–325.

42. *Ibid.*, sec. 327.

43. *Ibid.*, sec. 341(a).

44. A "point" is an origination fee of 1 percent, or one point, charged to the loan applicant at the time the loan is issued.

45. In some instances borrowers were willing to pay over ten points in order to secure a loan.

46. When an S & L makes a loan, it can charge "points" to the borrower and these points are recorded as earned income at the time the loan is issued. If an S & L makes an "investment," no points can be charged because there is no borrower involved in the transaction.

47. S & Ls were willing to pay higher than market rates to secure funds because they needed these funds in order to make the large ADC loans.

48. *Rules and Regulations for Savings and Loan Associations*, promulgated November 15, 1963 by the Building and Loan Section of the Finance Commission of Texas and the Savings and Loan Commissioner of Texas (as amended July 16, 1979), sec. 8.1B.

49. *Ibid.*, sec. 8.1B(V).

50. *Rules and Regulations* (as amended March 3, 1981), sec. 2.3.

51. *Ibid.*, sec. 2.11.

52. *Rules and Regulations* (as amended October 28, 1981), sec. 8.1(B).

53. *Ibid.*, sec. 8.1(D).

54. Interview with Art Leiser, director of examinations, Texas Savings and Loan Department, Austin, November 17, 1986.

55. Real estate owned is an asset that arises when an S & L acquires property after borrowers default on their loans.

56. This 100 percent loan limit was one reason for the failure of Empire S & L of Mesquite, Texas.

57. *Rules and Regulations* (as amended March 31, 1981), sec. 9.10.

58. *Ibid.*, sec. 9.11.

59. *Ibid.*, sec. 9.13.

60. The Empire S & L case was featured on the television program "60 Minutes." This brought much public attention to the Texas S & L industry.

61. *Hearing: Adequacy of FHLBB Supervision of Empire Savings and Loan Association*, Committee on Government Operations, House of Representatives, 98th Congress, 2d session, April 25, 1984, p. 77.

62. *House Report: FHLBB Supervision and Failure of Empire Savings and Loan Association of Mesquite, Texas*, Forty-fourth report by the Committee on Government Operations, August 6, 1984, p. 66.

63. John Yang, "Failed S & L Accounted for an Investment as Loan to Hide Loss, Bank Board Says," *Wall Street Journal*, September 15, 1986, p. 8.

64. *Hearing: Adequacy of FHLBB Supervision*, p. 2.

65. *Ibid.*, p. 21.

66. *Ibid.*

67. *House Report: FHLBB Supervision*, p. 21.

68. *Ibid.*, p. 14.

69. *Hearing: Adequacy of FHLBB Supervision*, p. 262.

70. Leon Wynter, "Study Says Regulators Slow to Address Faulty Appraisals for Bank, S & L Loans," *Wall Steet Journal*, December 13, 1986, p. 6.

71. "Savings Firms Face Problems From Land Loans—FBI Banking Investigators are Reviewing Transactions," *Dallas Morning News*, December 5, 1983.

72. *House Report: FHLBB Supervision*, p. 2.

73. *Ibid.*, p. 53.

74. In 1985 the Rules and Regulations for Texas Savings and Loan Associations were rewritten with the emphasis on giving the S & L commissioner expanded powers in dealing with troubled S & Ls.

75. *Fifty-Fourth Annual Report of Savings and Loan Associations*, Texas Savings and Loan Department in cooperation with Texas Savings and Loan League, 1982.

76. *Ibid.*

77. *FSLIC-Insured Savings and Loan Associations Combined Financial Statements* (Washington, D.C., Federal Home Loan Bank Board, 1982).

78. *Fifty-Fourth Annual Report of Savings and Loan Associations*.

79. John Crockett and Thomas King, "The Contribution of New Asset Powers to S & L Earnings: A Comparison of Federal and State-Chartered Associations in Texas," *FHLBB Research Working Paper No. 110*, July 1982, p. 1.

80. *Ibid.*, p. 3.

81. Interview with Jack Cashin, former executive vice president of the Texas S & L League, Austin, October 15, 1986.

6

The Second Crisis of the 1980s: National and Texas S & Ls, 1983—88

For the second time in this decade the U.S. thrift industry is in crisis. Once again the collective performance of S & Ls is deteriorating, institutional failures are numerous and widespread, and industry regulators—uncertain as anyone else about the future—are buried in paperwork. But this time the difficulties are more complex, and their resolutions more costly, than was the case in the early 1980s.

In this chapter we explore the roots of this crisis by looking at the industry from several angles in an attempt to ascertain whether the current reform effort is viable. Specifically, we chronicle the industry's history from July 1986 through June 1988—the two years of serious backsliding for most of the nation's thrifts. In these pages we try to present, as fairly as possible, the story of this incredible decline, one so pervasive that, as of this writing, much of the industry rests on the brink of insolvency. Included is an examination of how reregulation, mergers, and the infusion of capital have charted the desired course of recovery for these embattled institutions.

The chapter's first section focuses on the industry's purely financial problems, including statistics related to net worth, after-tax income, insolvencies, and undercapitalization. The next section addresses the reasons for the dramatic turnaround from the apparently prosperous 1983–86 era to the current disaster. Here we pay special attention to the controversial "time-bomb" loans, deposit insurance, and the handling of deposits by insolvent thrifts. Section three is an examination of the major proposals for reform, some of which have been implemented, designed to enable the industry to weather the crisis. The fourth section looks specifically at the legal and regulatory changes enacted during the years 1983–88. The final section offers a rundown of the innovations generated from within the industry, which constitute its current reform effort. Basically, these are standards and regulations aimed at straightening out the most troubled thrifts, and guiding the entire industry into another era of prosperity.

FINANCIAL PROBLEMS: U.S. AND TEXAS S & Ls

It's important to note at the outset of this section that the financial problems of U.S. S & Ls and those of Texas S & Ls are far from mutually exclusive—especially when examining losses. That is, in 1988 Texas thrifts led the nation in insolvencies, mergers (completed and proposed), and outright losses. This is not to say that Texas is the source of all national industry woes. Nor is it to suggest that the aforementioned leadership role Texans played among U.S. thrifts was a failure. It is, instead, to emphasize the central role of Texas S & Ls in the current crisis, and to point out why, and how, the fortunes of Texas thrifts mirror those of the nation's giant thrift industry.

The last time the S & L industry showed a collective profit was in the first quarter of 1987. Since then, each quarter's losses have exceeded those of the previous quarter.[1] In 1988's first quarter the loss total reached an all-time high: $3.8 billion. Of that total, $3.5 billion—more than 90 percent—was absorbed by Texas' 279 S & Ls.[2] The problems facing Texas thrifts were not unusual, but extreme; the losses suffered by these institutions were unusually high.

The industry's after-tax income, which peaked (an all-time high profit) at nearly $4 billion in 1985, declined to about $100 million the following year. But in 1987 the floor fell through, as institutions *lost* about $7 billion. Considering the level of S & L loss in the first quarter of 1988, fiscal year 1988 appears headed for record-level losses.

As for net worth, the picture looks equally bleak. One valuable measure of an institution's financial well-being is its net worth as a percentage of its assets. Nationally, S & Ls showed a combined net worth that was 4.4 percent of assets in 1985 and 4.6 percent in 1986 (this strange development—an increase in net worth accompanied by a decline in income—will be explained later in the chapter). But by 1987 the industry's net worth had dropped to 3.8 percent of assets.[3] As their troubles continue, S & Ls very likely will see a further reduction in 1988, due in part to "write-downs"[4] and in part to new regulations governing the determination of net worth.[5] However, the main factor contributing to this phenomenon is the ever-increasing number of insolvent thrifts—particularly in Texas.

Insolvencies themselves are a great concern to government (which may be asked to bail out failed thrifts and rescue stranded depositors) and to the industry (which risks losing face with consumers) as a whole. For the first quarter of 1988, though, neither government nor the S & L industry could stop the flood of failures nationwide. In those three long months 504 thrifts became, or remained, insolvent.[6] Of these, 130 were located in Texas, meaning that nearly one-half of its S & Ls were technically without any net worth.[7]

The insolvency problem, as bad as it is for the affected thrifts themselves, is especially painful to the industry. That is, even though these institutions remain broke, their doors, in most cases, stay open. In the process, huge losses are incurred—losses that reflect very badly, and, it seems just to say, unfairly, on the industry as a whole—that cannot be blamed on the mismanagement, gambling, and misfortune of a relatively few associations. Moreover, according to Representative Charles Schriner (D-N.Y.), the industry is losing $30 million a *day* simply because of the *delays in closing* these sick thrifts.[8] Consequently, the industry finds itself falling deeper in debt. This problem, most analysts agree, must be reconciled—through closures, mergers, or a combination thereof—before the national industry can hope to again enjoy an era of prosperity.

A major problem afflicting these troubled S & Ls is the high cost of securing funds. Indeed, many of these thrifts continue to pay 100 to 150 basis points more than the average thrift for deposits.[9] In order to attract new funds these insolvent or troubled thrifts offer these higher deposit rates. These increased costs, in most cases, lead to continued and growing losses.

In addition to the high cost of funds, these failing and near-failing S & Ls face another serious problem, one involving holdings of real estate. While this is an industry-wide problem, it is especially acute among financially strapped institutions. Still, for the industry nationwide, the Real Estate Owned assets totaled only $7.8 billion in 1983. By 1986, however, the figure had swelled to $20 billion, and by the end of 1987 it had climbed to over $24 billion.[10] Why is this a problem? Because, as explained earlier in the book, such assets are non-income-earning. That is, they are assets to the institution but provide no real income to the S & L. So with overall net worth down, and non-income-earning holdings up, the chances for quick recovery seem minimal. However, most industry observers suggest that, when the cost of deposits declines, and the level of Real Estate Owned likewise drops, a major recovery should follow.

Again, it is pointless to attempt to separate Texas from the nation as a whole when discussing S & L fortunes. Since the 1960s Texas thrifts have paved the way for the rest of the nation's thrifts by introducing new asset and liability instruments, taking numerous chances, and giving institutions more freedom generally. As a result, when Texas S & Ls have experienced good times, those following their lead have likewise enjoyed success. However, since no other state went so far in its liberalization of S & L laws and regulations as did Texas, none realized the impressive level of profits boasted by Texas-based thrifts, particularly in the 1970s. Similarly, none were hit as hard as Texas by the crises of the 1980s.

As mentioned earlier, about one-half of Texas' thrifts are at this time insolvent, and the state's 279 institutions suffered a loss of approximately $3.5 billion in the first quarter of 1988.

Also troubling these S & Ls is their newly acquired repossessions. Indeed, in 1987 after nine months of financial misery repossessed assets among Texas thrifts totaled $7.1 billion—nearly double the figure from the beginning of the year. With this accumulation, repossessed assets then amounted to more than 7 percent of all assets held by Texas S & Ls—a percentage far in excess of that found in any other states' industry. What's more, industry experts maintain that repossession totals among Texas thrifts are continuing to increase.[11]

Another important measure of S & L health is the number of home foreclosures. Statistics on homes financed via the Veteran's Administration reveal that, at the end of the first quarter in 1988, over one-third of the VA's inventory was located in Texas.[12] Indeed, Texas by that time featured 7,316 VA-foreclosed homes, worth a total of $315 million. By way of comparison, the state with the second-highest level of VA foreclosures, Colorado, had suffered only 2,124 such repossessions, amounting to $91 million.[13]

A final gauge by which the financial posture of S & Ls may be measured is that of simple net worth. For Texas thrifts, this statistical category may be sufficient to convince anyone of their collective plight. In 1984 the state's industry enjoyed a net worth as a percentage of assets of 3.8 percent. By 1986 it had declined to .54 percent, and in 1987 it hit a low of −6.2 percent.[14]

It is not difficult to see why, when government focuses on the ailing thrift industry in the United States, it turns first to Texas. Accordingly, the FHLBB has targeted states of the Southwest, and Texas in particular, in its strategy for S & L recovery. Specifically, the Board has pinpointed these states as those most in need of programs for bringing about S & L merger, liquidation, or consolidation of their faltering thrifts. Thus, as with the national recovery in general, all eyes will be fixed on Texas as these programs (discussed shortly) proceed.

CAUSES OF THE SECOND CRISIS

This second crisis, like the first, can be traced to 1979, when Paul Volcker, determined to lower the national rate of inflation, restricted the money supply. This restriction raised the cost of borrowing, as interest rates soared. For S & Ls (and other financial institutions), this caused the cost of funds to exceed the asset yield on loans. This caused the first crisis, prompting thrifts to seek new means of earning income. In response, the federal government made available, through deregulation, some new revenue sources. Simply stated, they made it possible for thrifts to issue non-home mortgage loans.

Many of these new loans, though risky, were attractive to S & Ls in desperate need of income. Specifically, they were most fond of the income earned on origination fees (discussed earlier). But the short-term "fix" for so many thrifts proved disastrous in the long run. That is, from 1983 until early 1986 the nation's S & Ls appeared in fine shape, particularly with respect to earnings. Since then, however, observers have sought explanations for the disastrous turnaround that has befallen these institutions. To be sure, much of this explanation lies in the "quick-fix" loans of the early 1980s.

As explained earlier, many of these high-risk, controversial loans were of the acquisition, development, and construction variety, and a high percentage of them featured 100 percent financing (or, in some cases, 100 percent-plus financing). The purpose of such novel loans was, simply, to generate income. So thrift accountants, as well as regulators, began to allow as income those fees and percentages charged to "book loans"— in real estate jargon, up-front "points." In the process (and the excitement), inflated appraisals of many projects (a rarity in times of S & L affluence) resulted in 100 percent-plus financing. In many cases of overappraisal, the excess funds were placed into "reserve accounts" to provide interest payments on the loans. Despite the fact that such interest payments were declared as income, involved thrifts were, in effect, paying themselves.[15]

Within the S & L industry many officials referred to these as "time-bomb" loans, because once the reserve account for one was exhausted the interest payments ceased, and the project was returned to the S & L. In addition to such loans, many thrifts loaned money to customers simply to cover their interest payments. The idea was that the original loan would exist as an income-producing asset—even though the "income" was being supplied by the S & L. Consequently, these types of loans fueled industry growth, as assets produced, for a few years, some income. However, once the "bombs" went off, such loans were abandoned; no new ones were made to cover interest changes. As a result, income statements and balance sheets worsened considerably.

Certainly not all S & Ls engaged in high-risk ventures, but the number of those undertaking such gambles is evidenced by the level of thrift insolvencies of the past few years. Indeed, an examination of the FSLIC's largest liquidations indicates the strong relationship between unsound lending practices and S & L failings. From the FSLIC's first major liquidation (of Empire S & L in 1984) to its most recent—and costly—of American Diversified Savings Bank of Costa Mesa, California, in 1988, the pattern is predictable. Empire, a modest thrift that, in mid-1982, had assets totaling $17 million, experienced an astronomical leap; in less than two years its assets were in excess of $300 million. Similarly, American Diversified realized inexplicable growth, from assets of approximately $11 million in mid-1983 to $792 million by the end of 1984. In each case ADC loans, and other risky loans, comprised the bulk of the thrifts' loan portfolios.[16] Moreover, it is apparent that ADC loans were a leading cause of 205 recent thrift insolvencies and, according to regulators, continue to exist as a major source of difficulty at numerous other S & Ls.[17]

Many observers, in examining the early years of the 1980s, place the blame for the late-1980s (second) crisis with the thrifts themselves, citing their aforementioned unsafe practices and lack of prudence in general as chief causes. However, in fairness it should be pointed out that, during these years of uncertainty, when thrifts were in dire need of quick income, thrift regulators regularly encouraged S & L investment in real estate development.[18]

The gap between the two crises of the 1980s—that is, the few prosperous in-between years—is further explained by a lack of regulatory control. Indeed, as the Reagan administration sought deregulation of the industry, it was of little surprise that the number of thrift examiners was reduced. This led to much of the untempered speculation by ambitious thrifts, and thus helped account for the short-lived S & L success of the mid-1980s.

By 1984, however, FHLBB head Edwin Gray, citing the industry's enormous rapid growth, requested through the Office of Management and Budget (OMB) 1,000 additional examiners. But a year later, when he finally received a response to his request, an OMB spokesman was blunt: "You don't understand the policy of this administration, which is that of deregulation. Deregulation means fewer examiners, not more."[19] To make matters worse, new examiners were, in 1984, paid paltry sums, a fact that doubtless led to subpar performances in many instances.

The shortage of examiners was especially acute in the five-state region of Texas, Arkansas, New Mexico, Louisiana, and Mississippi. Yet these areas featured more troubled S & Ls than any other in the nation; hence, the 116 examiners assigned to patrol the region's 510 thrifts were grossly overworked. "Essentially," said a senior vice president of the FHLBB of Dallas, "we were checkers of boxes."[20]

So, with rapid growth (due mostly to speculation and unfounded optimism) and a shortage of examiners, many loans of marginal quality went unnoticed. By 1986, however, examiners were acutely aware of this problem and its pervasiveness in the industry. They responded by forcing institutions with many of these dangerous loans outstanding to set aside, from current income, huge reserves as a buffer against potential losses. This action left many thrifts insolvent, as it resulted in tremendous net-worth losses.

What was the net effect of the clamp-down on adventurous S & Ls? In the short run, it meant many immediate insolvencies, and consequently a slowdown in marginal loan practices. This probably was good, however, as in the long run most of these thrifts were destined to collapse beneath the weight of these ill-conceived loans; the industry's overall losses stemming from imprudence, then, almost certainly were reduced, thanks to the examiners' seemingly harsh imposition.

Still, by late 1986 few doubted that the unsound lending practices of the early years of the decade were about to exact a heavy toll on the national S & L industry. For the second time, then, analysts wondered whether thrifts across the nation could survive the decade. Specifically, they wondered what would—

or could—be done to rescue hundreds of imperiled institutions, those whose ongoing operations were the cause of ever-increasing debt.

Inasmuch as the FHLBB and the FSLIC lacked sufficient funds to close all insolvent S & Ls, many continued to operate throughout 1987 and 1988. This in turn created additional problems, for healthy thrifts in particular. Besides giving the industry a shaky public image, the continued operations of these debt-ridden associations led the FSLIC to impose an *additional* insurance charge of one-eighth of 1% on all thrifts, for the purpose of subsidizing liquidations and mergers of troubled institutions. This "surcharge" was substantial, as the regular charge for FDIC or FSLIC insurance was only one-twelfth of 1%.[21]

To the ailing thrifts this insurance premium hike was welcomed for obvious reasons: it cost very little, compared to their ongoing losses, and it offered the possibility of rescue. To financially fit S & Ls this increase represented a subsidization of the industry's least competitive, most imprudent members, and, of course, it raised the cost of doing business for all thrifts.

Another problem awaiting healthy and unhealthy S & Ls alike was that of waning consumer confidence. Indeed, by the 1980s Americans had become extremely conscious of product quality. Now, with almost daily reports of S & L failures appearing in newspapers, many consumers were thinking twice about depositing their hard-earned money in high-risk financial institutions. Consequently, thrifts, even financially sound ones, were forced to increase the interest rates on deposits in order to attract new customers and retain established ones.

As one might expect, due to their inordinately high insolvency rate, Texas thrifts were hit harder by customer abandonment than were other associations throughout the nation. In order to compensate, these institutions, in the first quarter of 1988, averaged paying on deposits 60 basis points more than the national S & L average.[22] But the "Texas Premium," as the interest bonus has come to be known, will cost the state's thrift industry over $500 million a year.[23]

The temptation to offer above-average rates on deposits is not restricted to Texas S & Ls, however. In California, the ill-fated American Diversified Savings Bank, the largest FSLIC-liquidated S & L in history, at the time of its closing was paying a whopping 150 basis points above the national average.[24] These and other faltering thrifts, relying on this desperate method of securing new deposits, forced other thrifts, solvent and insolvent alike, to raise their deposit rates as well. Accordingly, this worked, and continues to work, to drive down industry profits.

Among industry officials, one popular argument has been that the increased cost of funds—or, viewed another way, the decrease in profits—among thrifts can be traced to the $100,000 deposit insurance limit on individual accounts. Since depositors who stay within this limit have nothing to fear, officials argue, they search for thrifts offering the most generous interest rates, and shift their business accordingly. Moreover, since insolvent S & Ls have a habit of offering the highest deposit rates, the result is a steady flow of funds from solvent institutions to their insolvent counterparts. Even though the insolvent thrifts are likely to fail eventually, officials maintain, the effect of their last-ditch efforts to survive is the same (indeed, it is no secret that some especially ambitious shoppers hunt down thrifts on the brink of closure, make deposits, wait for collapse, and redeposit in *other* teetering institutions). The net impact of the high insurance limit, S & L officials contend, is increased business costs, a cut in profits industry-wide, along with a steadily worsening financial picture for all.

An additional factor contributing to declining profitability among thrifts involves regulations in accounting practices. Historically the S & L industry has used regulatory accounting practices (RAP), but recently, due to a series of regulatory changes, the industry has moved in the direction of uniform usage of generally accepted accounting practices (GAAP). This is significant because the RAP system is more liberal in recognizing income and assets.[25] For example, one change involves income derived from loan origination fees. Suppose that on a given loan an S & L charges four points. Under RAP, it has the option of applying a portion of the charge—perhaps two points—to current income and amortizing the rest. But under GAAP the entire charge—in this example, all four points—must be amortized over the life of the loan. Needless to say, this is causing a substantial reduction in current income—at a time when profits already are low.

PROPOSALS FOR A HEALTHY FUTURE

By 1986 the greatest danger facing most U.S. S & Ls no longer involved the mismatching of assets and liabilities; by that time such difficulties paled next to the problem of bad loans, and the related horror of rapidly declining net worth. These loans, most of which were made in the early 1980s for the express purpose of providing up-front income as a means of offsetting losses resulting from an inverted yield curve, thus became the focal point of industry officials and regulators alike.

As a temporary means of avoiding bankruptcy, such loans, though risky on the surface, seemed worth making; but when overdue notes on these obligations became commonplace, the thrift industry was gripped by fear. Moreover, the problem was compounded as S & Ls began to fail under the weight of these loans. With such an unusually higher number of institutional failures, the FSLIC was under enormous pressure. In fact, by the end of 1986 the body's reserve funding had dropped to a negative $6.3 billion.[26]

Since S & L failures involve, in almost all instances, a bail-out by the FSLIC and FHLBB, the incentive to straighten out industry problems is a prime concern of regulators. Therefore, several proposals for brightening the future of S & Ls are aimed at strengthening the posture of those agencies of government charged with keeping the industry healthy and profitable, as we shall see.

One such proposal involves tying insurance premiums on loans to the risk posed by the particular loan type, or to the size of the loan-granting institution. Under a specific proposal of this type made by the FDIC, insured institutions would be given "risk ratings," based on asset quality, interest-rate risk, and capital adequacy.[27] The idea is to promote prudent behavior by S & Ls, encouraging them to develop thoughtful investment strategies. However, while most analysts agree that this is a reasonable means of averting many future S & L problems, they argue that it does not address the more weighty, immediate problem: surviving the plethora of bad loans *currently* on thrifts' books.

A second, more ambitious reform proposal would consolidate both insurance agencies, the FDIC and the FSLIC. In theory, this would establish a single agency more potent than either currently in existence. Indeed, while the reserves of each agency seem modest (given the gravity of the problem of bad loans), their combined assets surely would strengthen the position of their S & L clients. One argument on behalf of such a merger, made by FDIC chairman William Isaac, is that newly realized S & L powers have nearly erased the distinction between banks and S & Ls.[28] On the other hand, many S & L officials oppose such a plan, as they take exception to Isaac's suggestion that thrifts enjoy powers comparable to those held by full-service banks. They see, therefore, no advantage in the proposal, as it would, in their eyes, give them a clear "backseat" to banks.[29]

A third proposal involves a scheme to enhance the posture of the FSLIC through recapitalization. Foremost among those advocating such a plan is Edwin Gray, who in 1986 introduced a proposal that would allow the Board to collect an additional fee, totaling 1 percent of deposits, from federally insured thrifts. This, he maintained, would give the agency an additional $8.5 billion, and would provide quick relief for ailing thrifts. However, as with the other reform proposals, Gray's plan has its critics. Among them is House Banking Committee Chairman Fernand St. Germain, who insists that the 1 percent plan "could push already-weakened institutions into the pit."[30] Furthermore, officials of healthy S & Ls have voiced objection to their being forced to bail out their weakened competitors.[31]

A more popular recapitalization proposal, one sought by both the Board and the Treasury Department, would raise new FSLIC funds. This plan involves using capital from the FHLBs to start a government corporation, one that would provide funds to the FSLIC from the proceeds of certain debt issues. This scheme would, according to the U.S. General Accounting Office, provide sufficient funds for the FSLIC to begin resolving the S & L industry's current problems.[32] Since this proposal was made, some recapitalization has in fact been provided.[33]

Another plan to bolster the standing of the FSLIC calls for

an alteration in auditing procedures by the regulatory agencies.[34] Traditionally, the practice of these agencies has been to reappraise all nonperforming loans, and follow up by establishing loss reserves and/or write-downs.[35] For many S & Ls, this has meant a reduction in the level of required operating capital. Consequently, this has resulted in numerous insolvencies and many bail-outs by the FSLIC—causing a serious drain of the agency's reserves.

Of course not all of the road to recovery can be paved by a better-financed government insurance plan. Other problems involving S & L operations must be addressed separately. One of these problems, discussed earlier, is that of overbuilding in the commercial real estate market, particularly in certain regions of the country. Because new tax laws have discouraged investors from continuing to purchase these completed projects, many have been turned back to S & Ls. These institutions are, then, stuck with overvalued assets, ready for reappraisal in markets already saturated. This results in write-downs and reductions in net worth.

When the commercial real estate market is distressed, there is a tendency for thrifts to attempt to unload such holdings, as their losses already have been booked. An institution with such excess property may assume that its best available option is to recover, through resale, as much cash as possible. But as more and more S & Ls pursue such a strategy, market values are driven down, as the supply of available properties grows.

In response to this problem, as well as the general capitalization problem, Dr. Joseph Ewers, consultant to the Texas Savings and Loan League, has proposed that a new set of regulatory policies be enacted. His plan calls for a system emphasizing the use of a "net present value" approach when considering the holding, or selling, of a given property. Under this system a property-holding thrift would estimate the cash-flow potential over a given holding period, discount the cash flow at a market capitalization rate, and then decide, based on comparative present values, whether to sell or hold the property.[36] For example, a holding period of five years could be established, with property cash-flow projections made on that basis. Then, a current capitalization rate—perhaps 10 percent—would be applied. With this formula it would be easy to compute the present value of the given property. If the discounted present value were to exceed the current market cash offer for the property, then the rational decision would be to hold onto the property for a time; but if the price exceeded the discounted present value, the property would be sold.[37]

Though Dr. Ewers does not see this as a cure-all proposal, he does view it as an important step in the direction of financial stability for many thrifts, and certainly a preferable alternative to the "fire sale" approach generally taken by S & Ls. Whether or not the Ewers proposal or another one is selected, most industry analysts, according to Art Leiser, director of examinations, Texas Savings and Loan Department, agree that some plan is needed to prevent the continuation of "distress" commercial property sales by so many thrifts.[38]

Another plausible reform proposal, mentioned earlier as a preference of many S & L officials, is a lowering of the $100,000 insurance limit. While such a move would benefit most directly the profitable thrifts, it would additionally serve to instill in depositors a keener sense of prudence as they make their savings decisions. The anticipated consequence of such a reform is a massive transfer of deposits, from weak institutions to healthy ones, as the fear of failure would, in the minds of most depositors, outweigh the marginal rate advantage offered by faltering S & Ls. (Of course it would be incumbent on depositors to ascertain the relative strength of a given thrift; in some cases, of course, fairly strong institutions might nevertheless be offering rates competitive with those available at struggling institutions, and consumers would want to be aware of such instances.) This scheme, while popular with many S & L leaders, is unlikely to materialize, as the U.S. government almost never retreats from its financial "guarantees," whether they be Social Security benefit levels, welfare payments, unemployment stipends, or, in this case, protection against unsafe savings investments.

A different sort of reform proposal, one with a distinct future orientation, is known as "risks control arbitrage." This involves the use of options and futures market investments by thrifts, a strategy currently employed by very few institutions. The advantage of such investment is that it effectively transfers interest-rate risk from S & Ls, who do not wish to accept it, to a sector of the economy far better-equipped to handle such uncertainty.[39] Indeed, S & Ls that in the past have relied on these markets have succeeded in decreasing interest-rate risks as well as some of the vulnerabilities inherent in their uneven asset/liability term structures.

A final proposal, one designed chiefly to halt the wild, last-ditch efforts by deeply troubled S & Ls, would place a ban on asset-growth by institutions that, under regulatory accounting rules, are insolvent. In addition, the plan would permit the FHLBB to force an annual *reduction* in the assets of badly insolvent thrifts whenever the Board has installed its own managers in such thrifts. The benefits of these growth restrictions are, first, that they would ease the interest-rate pressure, brought to bear by insolvent S & Ls, on the industry's healthier associations; and second, that they would simply reduce the industry's rate of increase in number of risky loans.

While others have suggested additional reforms, the aforementioned proposals have met with the most serious consideration, by industry officials and government alike. While there is much disagreement as to which reforms are most desirable, few analysts are quick to dismiss all of them as unsuitable or undesirable. This is because, quite simply, the S & L industry needs help, and quickly. Besides these ideas, efforts to straighten out the troubled thrift industry have involved numerous regulatory reforms. The following section explores the nature of such reforms and their impact on the industry.

U.S. GOVERNMENT REGULATION, 1983–88

Federal regulatory changes involving thrifts following the initial industry crisis of the 1980s came in two waves, from 1983 to 1986 and from early 1986 to 1988. It was during the first period of change that the Reagan administration successfully "deregulated" the industry—that is, liberalized the laws and regulations governing federal S & Ls. The second period, as we shall see, represented a return to government reregulation, though such reform took on a new character.

By 1983 the federal government was determined to assist the national thrift industry in its struggle for survival through enactment of a series of key regulatory changes. First, in January of that year, the interest-rate ceilings on short-term accounts with minimum balances of $2,500 (i.e., 7- to 31-day and "Super NOW" accounts, and 91-day and 26-week MMCs) were eliminated. Three months later, certificates of two and one-half years or more were no longer subject to interest-rate ceilings or minimum balance requirements. Six months later, in October, interest-rate ceilings on deposits with maturities or notice periods of more than 31 days, and on deposits of at least 7 days with $2,500 minimum balances, were eliminated.[40]

The following year, 1984, again witnessed a tremendous liberalization of the thrift industry. In January the minimum amount for deposits that were exempt from interest-rate ceilings was reduced, from $2,500 to $1,000. Finally, in March 1986, the 5.5 percent ceiling on passbook accounts was lifted. This final freedom represented the last phase of S & L deregulation. It was followed by termination of the six-year-old DIDC.[41]

Of further significance to thrifts was the future of their net-worth certificates (NWCs) which, for several years, had helped numerous thrifts avoid insolvency. Again, government came to the rescue, as in February 1983 the FSLIC made a commitment to purchase NWCs from an institution once the institution had made an initial purchase. These certificates, once exchanged for FSLIC promissory notes, became eligible for inclusion in regulatory net-worth totals—thereby bolstering the capital position of S & Ls holding them. Moreover, in September 1984 the initial assistance level for securing NWCs was raised, and certain requirements were simplified for thrifts seeking FSLIC assistance through the NWC program.[42]

During this same period of regulatory activity, net-worth requirements themselves underwent noteworthy change. In 1983 S & Ls were required to maintain net-worth positions equaling at least 3 percent of their liabilities. But in March 1985 the standard was altered drastically, in order to ensure that rapidly growing institutions remained well-capitalized. However, the new requirements were tied strictly to institutional *growth*. For example, if an S & L grew at an annual rate of 15 percent or less, the net worth requirement remained at 3 percent of any liability growth. If the association grew at a rate of 15–25 percent, the net worth requirement was to be calculated on a graduated scale, ranging from 3 to 5 percent of liability growth. For an institution with annual growth in excess of 25 percent, the requirement held at 5 percent of liability growth. Finally, S & Ls were notified that, whenever their assets exceeded $100 million, the FHLBB had to grant permission for annual growth in excess of 25 percent.[43]

Another change of great significance, stemming from the Empire case in Texas, involved requirements for new ownership. In August 1984 the FSLIC established new, stricter requirements for the selection of directors and managers of newly organized S & Ls. The purpose of these lofty standards was the avoidance of conflict-of-interest problems among new owners. Similar rules were adopted for the handling of acquisitions of converted institutions. These provided, among other things, that changes in control of the stock of newly converted, insured institutions would be restricted for three years.[44]

The federal government added two other critical components to its earliest effort to assist S & Ls. First, in February 1983 the FHLBB streamlined the procedures required for a mutual S & L to convert to a stock institution. This spawned an increase in the number of conversions among mutual associations, thereby allowing these new stock associations to raise capital via stock sales.[45] Then, in May 1983, Congress passed a law preempting any state law restricting lenders' rights to exercise due-on-sale clauses. This would surely cause a number of marginal, low-rate mortgages to be repaid, as they could not be assumed by their purchasers; new mortgages, of course, generally would carry higher interest rates. The net effect of this federal law, then, was beneficial to most thrifts, as it rid them of many old, low-interest mortgages.[46]

By 1985, following a sense of adjustments within the S & L industry nationwide, the FHLBB announced two important changes in thrift practices involving direct investments and loan classifications. First, in March, the Board called on the FSLIC to begin requiring S & Ls to post 10 percent reserves against all direct investments made after December 10, 1984, but only if such investments exceeded the greater of 10 percent of an institution's assets or twice its regulatory net worth. This would prevent a thrift from possessing a large number of risky direct-investment assets in its portfolio without a substantial reserve as backup help in the event of heavy defaults.[47]

Next, in December of that year, the examiners of FSLIC-insured savings institutions were permitted to classify questionable loans, and other assets, for purposes of requiring general and specific reserve allocations. These examiners were given new loan categories, such as those dubbed "loss," "doubtful," and "substandard." The new classification scheme gave the examiners more realistic choices in deciding upon categorization for purposes of loan repayment possibilities. Many, including Texas S & L Department Chief Examiner Art Leiser, believe that this new system gave the thrift industry one of its greatest boosts.[48]

Generally speaking, the S & L recovery period of 1983–86 can be characterized as one focusing on troubled institutions. Indeed, the aforementioned legal and regulatory changes enacted during these years were designed for the express purpose of assisting those thrifts featuring low earnings and/or low net worth. Basically, the idea was to minimize the possibility of future unprofitability for these and other S & Ls. But the second phase of government-sponsored thrift reform has been, as we shall now see, one aimed at straightening out the entire industry, not simply those institutions flirting with failure.

In March 1986, when the 5.5 percent ceiling on passbook accounts finally was lifted, savings deregulation had been accomplished.[49] This freedom was coupled with the promise of increased after-tax income later that year, when Congress passed the landmark Tax Reform Act. This helped thrifts by reducing the top corporate tax rate from 46 to 34 percent. However, it also lowered, from 40 to 8 percent, the maximum deduction on taxable income stemming from bad debts.[50]

By October 1986 the FHLBB toughened its stand on thrift loans, by requiring stricter record-keeping. This new regulation required all savings institutions to establish records for commercial and consumer loans; under the former system only loans secured by real estate were so regulated.[51]

As important as the reforms of 1986 were, the Competitive Equality Banking Act of 1987 was the most influential legislation passed in the late 1980s. This comprehensive piece of legislation, passed by Congress following much debate, is unique in that it covers several different types of S & L activities. Its overall purpose, clearly, was to rescue troubled thrifts and minimize the financial woes of healthier ones.

First, the law authorized a $10.8 billion recapitalization/bonding program for the FSLIC. Next, it approved supervisory forebearance of up to three years for well-managed, capital-weak thrifts in economically depressed areas. These provisions are especially beneficial to marginally strong S & Ls, as they offer specific government protection against "life-threatening" financial downturns.[52]

All thrifts are affected by the 1987 law as its other major provisions necessarily apply more evenly. For one thing, it provided a schedule for the phase-out of the aforementioned "special" FSLIC premium assessments. Furthermore, the act established a one-year moratorium on converting from FSLIC to FDIC insurance. Finally, the landmark piece of federal legislation simplified the process of restructuring troubled loans and the maximization of recoveries on such loans.[53]

Later in 1987 the FHLBB again acted, this time amending the definition of regulatory capital and altering accounting principles, regulations, and procedures, so as to bring the accounting standards of thrift institutions more into line with those already used by banks. As a result, all thrifts eventually must report virtually all components of regulatory capital in accordance with GAAP.[54] The short-term impact of this important procedural change will be a reduction in the net worth of most thrifts. Over the longer haul, however, the new system is certain to present a more accurate account of the capital position of thrifts nationwide.

In June 1988, Danny Wall, FHLBB chairman, announced that the special FSLIC premium charged S & Ls, scheduled for phase-out, would likely be extended through 1995.[55] Then, in July 1988, Wall announced another extension, this time through 1998.[56] Already this has compelled officials of strong S & Ls to seriously consider shifting insurance to the FDIC.

Also in 1988, Congress announced that the one-year moratorium on conversion from FSLIC to FDIC insurance, scheduled to end in August 1988, would be extended one additional year.[57] This action is expected to have the effect of motivating strong S & Ls to stick with the FSLIC, as the premium rates will be shared by all thrifts.

As these laws and regulations continue to alter the course of S & L activity throughout the nation, analysts debate whether more, fewer, or different regulations would best serve the industry. Apart from legal changes, the nation's thrifts have undergone sweeping change since 1982—a year in which many analysts were predicting the total collapse of the nation's S & L industry. We now turn to an examination of the reform effort from a broader perspective with primary focus on change generated from within the industry.

RECOVERY AND REFORM: A NEW INDUSTRY ON THE HORIZON

Since an aura of depression enveloped the U.S. thrift industry in 1982, certain things have happened to suggest that the S & L industry *could* be a viable and profitable industry. Basically, several steps have been taken in the pursuit of reversing the fundamental imbalance in the asset and liability structures of thrifts, and in helping them raise new capital. These efforts, plus a decline in interest rates between 1983 and 1986, set the stage for a serious chance of recovery in the final years of the decade.[58]

One of the positive signs of a return to S & L profitability during the mid-1980s was reflected in the industry's after-tax net income. In both 1981 and 1982 S & Ls nationwide lost in excess of $4 billion. But the years 1983–85 produced steady growth as well as positive after-tax income (in each of the three years). Indeed, in 1985 net income after taxes neared the all-time industry high of $4 billion.[59]

Another positive sign of the industry's renewed strength is its collective net worth situation. In 1982 the industry hit a modern net-worth low of just under $26 billion; by mid-1986, however, this figure had risen to over $50 billion. Moreover, in

1982 net worth as a percentage of liabilities plummeted to less than 3.5 percent; four years later it was up to nearly 4.7 percent.[60]

For many industry analysts one of the most important turnarounds achieved by S & Ls involved the return on average assets. Following two years of negativity—1981 and 1982—a positive average return on assets was recorded for the industry. While 1981 saw a low of negative .73 percent, by 1985 this number increased to a positive .4 percent return—fairly good by historical standards.[61] This was a very promising sign for the future, because as S & Ls are able to overcome their bad-loan problem—involving, mainly, those issued in the early 1980s—their return on average assets should rise a great deal more.

Two final signs of S & L health involve their long-term prospects for growth, and both are very promising. First is the spread between the average cost of funds and the average portfolio yield. Across the nation, the industry actually experienced a negative spread (i.e., the cost of funds exceeded the portfolio yield) in the early 1980s. Since then, however, the spread among thrifts nationwide has become positive, growing steadily through 1986.[62] Second is the total number of mortgage loans closed annually. Between 1981 and 1986 the number of loans closed increased each year, and during those years the increase in such closures rose 280 percent.[63] Although the industry did turn around between 1982 and 1986, the tough times of the 1980s were not over and the once positive signs turned negative again as new problems faced the industry.

Because of industry losses incurred in 1981–82, the next four years represented a challenging era in S & L history as institutions were forced to find new ways to secure quick income. As we have seen, many thrifts turned to highly risky investments in order to remain solvent. But since then, many sectors of the economy—oil, agriculture, and some parts of "high-tech" in particular—have fallen on rough times. Consequently, thrifts have suffered as construction based on anticipated continued growth in these parts of the economy resulted in tremendous overbuilding in many regions of the country. With this overbuilding has come a depressed real estate market, and thrifts have found themselves holding a great many repossessed properties. Indeed, one of the most important challenges facing the thrift industry over the next few years will be its ability to hold onto these properties until the real estate market turns around. Otherwise, they will incur huge losses, from which many very likely will not recover.

The second crisis of the 1980s, related closely to the first, alerted the national government that help was needed if the industry was to survive. Such recognition meant assisting healthy thrifts generally, and bailing out others. In addition, it necessarily meant covering the losses incurred by failed thrifts.

As the FSLIC bailed out one insolvent thrift after another in the mid-1980s, its reserves dwindled appreciably: at the end of 1985 its reserve fund was $4.6 billion;[64] a year later it was a negative $6.3 billion.[65] Because of losses climbing steadily throughout 1986, the FSLIC ended the year technically bankrupt. Indeed, 1987 was no better when the fourth quarter of the year alone saw the agency's capital fall more than $2.7 billion, leaving the insurance fund a negative net worth in excess of $13 billion.[66]

By this time, however, many in government were busily preparing ways to refund the FSLIC. One of the first steps taken in 1985 was an FHLBB-sponsored special assessment rate of one-eighth of 1% of insured deposits (on top of the existing rate of one-twelfth of 1%) held by S & Ls. This assessment has raised, since its enactment, about $1.2 billion annually. These funds were earmarked, first, to replenish the FSLIC's reserve fund, and, later, to pay interest on bonds issued to recapitalize the fund.[67] Obviously, this has not been nearly sufficient to replace the major portion of funds lost.

Another important step taken, this time by Congress, in August 1987 was authorization for the sale of bonds, totaling $10.8 billion, to help recapitalize the S & L insurance fund. The scheme involves the sale of 30-year bonds over a three-year period.[68] To finance these bonds, the nation's remaining thrifts are being assessed additional charges. Thus, in the first half of 1988 the fund had borrowed $2.9 billion of the $10.8 billion total.[69] (The plan is that about $3.6 billion will be raised annually through these sales; therefore, only $.7 billion more would be available through 1988.)

Significant to note about this massive insurance fund bail-out is the targeting of collected monies. That is, a large portion of the initial $2.9 billion went into the FHLBB's "Southwest Plan," the aim of which was to consolidate insolvent thrifts—mostly those located in Texas and other southwestern states—with healthy associations. This merger plan was intended to end the insolvencies while eliminating overbanking in these states. Indeed, an important goal by sponsors of the plan was to reduce the number of Texas-based thrifts from 279, with 1,800 branches, to 160, with 1,400 branches. In addition, regulators expect the plan to attract new investors, with fresh capital—a development sure to strengthen the management of consolidated institutions.[70]

The first step in the "Southwest Plan" came on May 13, 1988, with the consolidation of five thrifts. This happened three months after thrift regulators had publicly outlined their S & L recovery plan. Still, many felt that the initial step took too long. However, FHLBB Chairman Danny Wall explained the delay: "The thrift situation in Texas is complex, and we want to be careful about how we put these consolidations together."[71]

Beyond this first step, although each subsequent consolidation is sure to differ from earlier ones, the basic plan is the same: the FSLIC infuses funds to cover the negative capital situation of the consolidated thrift.[72] In some cases infused funds will provide interest on non-income-earning assets for a period of time. This allows the S & L to hold onto the assets and realize earnings on them until such time as the market turns around. At that point, the assets may be sold profitably. The profits would be shared by the thrift and the FSLIC.

As these consolidations multiply, many of the institutions paying depositors the highest rates of interest will (ideally) be merged with healthier ones, and the rates, correspondingly, could be expected to decline. This rate savings alone is being counted on, by regulators and S & L officials alike, to save the industry billions of dollars annually.[73] Indeed, such a savings should, by itself, *help* return the ailing industry to profitability.

Along with recapitalizing plans, the FSLIC has been forced to liquidate many thrifts since the start of the industry's "second crisis." One day alone, in fact, the agency committed $1.35

billion to the liquidation of two Costa Mesa, California, S & Ls. Thus on June 6, 1988, the FSLIC spent $1.14 billion to clear out American Diversified Savings Bank—at that time the largest S & L liquidation in U.S. history.[74]

However, regulators hope to resolve most of Texas' problems, the nation's most severe, without resorting to liquidation. Most of the time, the FSLIC will seek buyers for failed thrifts as an alternative to liquidation, as the cost of the latter is much higher than that of recapitalization.

Another recent FHLBB tactic, launched in June 1988, has been dubbed by some observers "McDeal." Thrift regulators, frustrated by slow progress in the selling of insolvent thrifts, decided to gamble by imitating the fast food business' strategy. In the "McDeal" plan the FHLBB identified 21 thrifts—all outside of the troubled Southwest—to be auctioned quickly.[75] The first of these "McDeal" transactions took place in August of 1988, less than three months after the FHLBB begin soliciting bids on these troubled S & Ls.[76]

The call for "McDeal" resulted from the fact that, during the first half of 1988, only 40 ailing thrifts were closed or merged; but for the year, the FHLBB had projected the total number to be about 200.[77] So, together with the "Southwest Plan," it is the hope of the Board that "McDeal" will speed up necessary mergers and closings, perhaps enough so that the goal of 200 will be met by year's end. As with every other effort aimed at reinvigorating the nation's thrift industry, these represent only a fraction of what is needed to succeed. For U.S. S & Ls, the road to full recovery will continue to be long and arduous— and without any guarantee of completion.

NOTES

1. Michael Weiss, "Thrifts Lose $3.8 billion," *The Dallas Morning News,* June 22, 1988, p. 1A.

2. *Ibid.*

3. *Savings Institutions Source Book* (Chicago: United States League of Savings Institutions, 1985–88).

4. A "write-down" occurs when an institution lowers the value of an asset on its balance sheet.

5. The S & L industry is moving away from the regulatory accounting practices (RAP) system of accounting toward the generally accepted accounting practices (GAAP). The GAAP system of accounting is less liberal than RAP when accessing what is included as net worth.

6. Robert E. Taylor, "Insured Thrifts Post a Deficit of $3.78 Billion," *Wall Street Journal*, June 22, 1988, p. 7.

7. Allen Pusey, "S & L: How they self-destructed," *The Dallas Morning News*, November 8, 1987, p. 1H.

8. Taylor, p. 7.

9. David B. Hilder, 2d Robert E. Taylor, "Federal Regulators Liquidate 2 Thrifts in California for Record $1.35 Billion," *Wall Street Journal*, June 6, 1988, p. 2. Many institutions are paying higher deposit rates—not to make new loans or other investments, but rather to pay interest on existing deposits and to keep their doors open.

10. *Savings Institutions Source Book*, 1984–88.

11. Kirk Ladendorf, "First half is brutal for S & Ls," *Austin American Statesman*, October 16, 1987, p. E1.

12. Since a large percentage of S & L assets are in home mortgages, it is useful to analyze the home-foreclosures of the VA.

13. "Foreclosures spreading, report shows," *The Dallas Morning News*, June 14, 1988, p. 12D.

14. *Federal Home Loan Bank Board Financial Report*, (Washington, D.C., December 31, 1987).

15. Pusey, p. 1H.

16. Hilder and Taylor, p. 2.

17. Michael Binstein, "Feds detail cost of S & L bailout," *Austin American Statesman*, May 1, 1988, p. A1.

18. Kirk Ladendorf, "Ultimate wheeler-dealer," *Austin American Statesman*, June 5, 1988, p. D4.

19. Pusey, p. 1H.

20. *Ibid.*

21. Robert E. Taylor, "Bank Board Refusal to Shrink, S & L Levy Elicits Complaints from Thrift Industry," *Wall Street Journal*, April 4, 1988, p. 25.

22. Kirk Ladendorf, "Bank, S & L deposit rates worry officials," *Austin American Statesman*, February 21, 1988, p. H1.

23. *Ibid.*

24. Hilder and Taylor, p. 2.

25. R. Dan Brumbaugh, Jr. and Andrew Carron, "Thrift Industry Crisis: Causes and Solutions," Brookings Papers on Economic Activity (Washington, D.C., 1987), p. 354. RAP net worth includes preferred

stock; permanent, reserve, or guaranty stock; paid-in surplus; qualifying mutual capital certificates, income capital, and net worth certificates; qualifying subordinate debentures; appraised equity capital; reserves; undivided profits; and net undistributed income. GAAP net
worth excludes from this list qualifying mutual capital certificates; income capital and net worth certificates; qualifying subordinated debentures; and appraised equity capital. GAAP net worth includes de-
ferred net gains (losses) on assets sold.

26. Robert Taylor, "FSLIC Deficit Nearly Doubled in 1987; Thrift
Rescues Could Cost $15.3 Billion," *Wall Street Journal*, April 19, 1988,
p. 10.

27. "Deposit Insurance Reform Proposed," *Savings Bank Journal*, June
1983, p. 9.

28. *Ibid.*

29. Edwin Gray, "Bank Board/Thrift Perspectives," *Federal Home Loan
Bank Board Journal*, May/June 1983, p. 7. Although the S & Ls have
gained expanded powers through the passage of such laws as the
DIDMCA and the Garn–St. Germain Act, in every case thrifts are limited to a percentage-of-assets for each type of asset power. Commercial banks are not so limited. Therefore many in the S & L industry
argue that thrifts are not the same as commercial banks.

30. Leon Wynter, "St. Germain Says House Won't Act to Aid FSLIC
Without Plan From White House," *Wall Street Journal*, November 7,
1985, p. 6.

31. *Ibid.*

32. Monica Langley, "FSLIC's Reserves Dropped $1.1 Billion Dur-
ing 1985, According to GAO Audit," *Wall Street Journal*, July 3, 1986,
p. 2.

33. In August 1987 President Reagan signed a $10.8 billion recapi-
talization program to help bail out the S & L industry.

34. The regulatory agencies for S & Ls are the FSLIC, FHLBB, and
state S & L departments.

35. A loss reserve is an account kept against bad debts. Write-downs
are a loss in value written against the S & L capital account when a
property is reassessed at a value lower than the value written on the
S & L's books.

36. Joseph Ewers, "Current Commentary," *Texas League Savings Account*, Austin, November/December 1986, p. 12.

37. *Ibid.*

38. Interview with Art Leiser, director of examinations, Texas Savings and Loan Department, Austin, November 17, 1986.

39. Eugene Guyon, "A Critical Review of the Savings and Loan

Industry," Professional Report, The University of Texas, 1983, p. 57.

40. *Savings Institutions Source Book*, 1983–86.

41. *Ibid.*

42. *Ibid.*

43. "Net Worth Requirements of Insured Institutions," *Federal Home Loan Bank Board Draft*, January 31, 1985, p. 1.

44. *Savings Institutions Source Book*, 1983–86.

45. *Ibid.*

46. *Ibid.*

47. *Ibid.* An S & L needs principal supervisory approval for any direct investments above 10 percent of their assets.

48. Interview with Art Leiser, director of examinations, Texas Savings and Loan Department, Austin, January 18, 1987. These new classifications are the same as the ones commercial banks have used for years.

49. *1987 Savings Institutions Source Book*, p. 69.

50. *Ibid.*, p. 68.

51. *Ibid.*, p. 69.

52. *1988 Savings Institutions Source Book*, p. 68.

53. *Ibid.*

54. *Ibid.*, p. 69.

55. Robert E. Taylor, "Bank Board Sharply Lifts Estimate on Costs of Ending Thrifts Crisis," *Wall Street Journal*, July 7, 1988, p. 3.

56. *Ibid.*

57. This ruling that does not allow S & Ls to switch from FSLIC to FDIC insurance for an additional year (until August 1989) was very important to the FSLIC. Many S & Ls would move to the FDIC to avoid the higher insurance charges of FSLIC. (Currently the FSLIC premiums are two and one-half times higher than FDIC premiums.) The biggest problem facing FSLIC is that the stronger S & Ls are the institutions that want to switch, leaving FSLIC with the weak and insolvent S & Ls. In order to receive FDIC coverage an institution must have a net worth to asset ratio of 6 percent. This would allow only those strong S & Ls, with above 6 percent net worth, to change to FDIC coverage.

58. Patrick Mahoney and Alice P. White, "The Thrift Industry in Transition," *Federal Reserve Bulletin*, (Washington, D.C., March 1985), p. I.

59. *1986 Annual Report to Members: United States League of Savings Institutions* (Chicago, 1986).

60. *Ibid.*

61. *1986 Savings Institutions Source Book.*

62. *1986 Annual Report to Members.*

63. *Ibid.*

64. *1988 Savings Institutions Source Book,* p. 63.

65. *Ibid.*

66. *Ibid.*

67. Robert Taylor, "Thrifts' Struggle is Becoming Darwinian," *Wall Street Journal,* July 5, 1988, p. 6.

68. "Officials express optimism over bond sale to aid FSLIC," *The Dallas Morning News,* October 1, 1987, p. 12D.

69. David La Gesse, "Regulators Starting S & L Liquidation," *The Dallas Morning News,* June 7, 1988, p. 1D.

70. *Federal Home Loan Bank Board News* (Washington, D.C., May 13, 1988), p. 1.

71. *Ibid.*

72. *Ibid.,* p. 5.

73. *Ibid.,* p. 3.

74. La Gesse, p. 1D.

75. Robert E. Taylor, "Bank Board Cooks Up Program Aimed at Speeding Up Disposal of Sick Thrifts," *Wall Street Journal,* June 17, 1988, p. 26.

76. Robert Taylor, "Bank Board Clears 10 Thrift Takeovers Requiring Aid Totaling $948.5 Million," *Wall Street Journal,* August 29, 1988, p. 2.

77. *Ibid.*

7

Reform in the Texas and National Savings and Loan Industries: Summary, Conclusions, and the Current Path

Since the early 1960s savings and loan associations have been the most volatile of all U.S. financial institutions. During this period the S & L community, while overcoming numerous obstacles, has blossomed into a trillion-dollar industry. This growth, largely a function of industry diversity and innovation, has changed forever the character of S & Ls. Indeed, while the first century of S & L activity was restricted almost entirely to the financing of homebuilding, recent growth has resulted from industry experimentation with an assortment of financial endeavors. The leadership for such experimentation came, in part, from Texas state-chartered S & Ls. Aided by liberalization of state laws and regulations, these institutions heralded an era of industry-wide innovation. In the preceding chapters of this book we described the development of the S & L industry, in Texas and nationwide, with a primary focus on the period 1950–88. The following is a synopsis of that historical development, and an overview of very recent trends in the industry.

The first U.S. S & Ls were created during the decade of the

1830s for the sole purpose of solving home-financing problems. These early associations, patterned after England's "building societies," existed as nonprofit institutions. The original form of ownership was called a "terminating plan," wherein each member would receive a loan; the association was terminated following issuance of the final loan. Over time this ownership form evolved into the "permanent stock plan," which is in effect to this day. Under this newer plan the institution operates without a tie between savers and borrowers, and the permanent stock is used as a buffer against loan losses.

From its early years through World War II—more than 100 years—the S & L industry enjoyed steady growth, except for a slight setback suffered during the 1930s Great Depression. After 1948 the industry experienced unprecedented levels of growth. This growth was realized through the use of very restricted portfolios, as associations borrowed through the use of short-term liabilities (mainly savings accounts) and lent via long-term assets (mainly housing mortgages). This mismatching of asset and liability maturities worked well in the 1940s and 1950s, but by the 1960s it emerged as a serious industry-wide problem, as high rates of inflation caused the cost of funds to rise above the rate of interest charged on long-term home mortgages. At that point it became clear to industry officials that S & Ls were in need of new asset and liability instruments. Texas state-chartered S & Ls, armed with greater legal flexibility and a host of fresh ideas, began showing the nation how certain new instruments could work.

Critical to the role of Texas S & Ls as industry innovator was the appointment of the state's first savings and loan commissioner, R. A. Benson, in 1961. With Benson's appointment the state's S & Ls gained formal independence from the Texas Banking Commissioner. By 1963 the state had adopted a new S & L code, with one unique, critically significant feature: it permitted the S & L commissioner to promulgate rules and regulations he thought necessary for the survival and growth of the industry, without so much as notifying the Texas Legislature. This power would, in the two decades to follow, prove vital to the state industry's national leadership role.

Throughout the 1960s Texas state-chartered S & Ls were permitted to engage in various commercial loans, consumer loans, and direct property investments. It was not until the 1980s, with enactment of the DIDMCA and the Garn–St. Germain Act, that federally chartered institutions could fully participate in such activities. To a very great extent, the Garn–St. Germain Act was patterned after rules that had governed Texas state-chartered S & Ls for nearly two decades.

In the early years of the 1980s the national S & L industry met with crisis, and many observers feared for the industry's very survival. At this time interest-rate risk, caused by short-term liabilities averaging more than two percentage points higher than returns received on mortgages, was the industry's main problem. Moreover, high interest rates triggered a national recession, the result of which was the worst housing slide in U.S. history. By 1982, as thrift institutions were disappearing at the rate of one per day, the national government took decisive action to combat this situation by passing the Garn–St. Germain Act. This piece of legislation, along with the DIDMCA (passed in 1980), helped spawn the recovery of the S & L industry. Basically, these acts permitted S & Ls the opportunity to engage in more short-term, profitable loan-making.

In the early 1980s the most popular of the new types of loans may have been acquisition, development, and construction loans, which provided S & Ls quick income during times when the threat of insolvency loomed. On the other hand, they were very risky investment; if an institution provided 100 percent of the funding on a project that could not be sold, the initial investors would relinquish the property to the lending institution, which would then be stuck with a non-income-earning asset.

Toward the end of 1982 such high-risk ventures as ADC loans became less attractive as interest rates began dropping and as the S & L industry once again experienced profitability. Nevertheless, while problems revolving around interest rates no longer plagued institutions, problems associated with bad loans did (and, as of this writing, still do). Many of these loans were made in the early years of the 1980s, when S & Ls felt compelled to engage in high-risk ventures in order to secure their short-term survival. As a result problem loans continue through 1988 to cause severe financial strains, not only for those institutions that had originated the loans, but also for the FSLIC, which insured most such institutions. Indeed, by December 1986 the FSLIC was bankrupt with a net worth position of negative $6.3 billion. The bankrupt insurance was left trying to insure an industry with assets in excess of $1 trillion. As of this writing, most financial analysts expect Congress to continue recapitalizing the FSLIC or possibly consolidating it with the FDIC.

Still, by 1986 the industry had succeeded in achieving a recovery with the average net worth position of S & Ls in the United States reaching 4.6 percent of their assets. Before this historic rebound could even be fully assessed, however, the industry was hit with its second major crisis of the decade—problem loans—a situation more threatening (at least in strict monetary terms) than the first. Since 1986, regulators and industry leaders have struggled to save U.S. thrift institutions.

Throughout 1987 and 1988 many articles were written about the woes of S & Ls. Writers pointed out that losses were continuing to climb, the FSLIC's negative worth position worsened, and cost estimates of an industry bail-out rose steadily. They remarked, with few dissenting opinions, that there was little reason to be optimistic about the industry's future.

By mid-1988 some of these authors, joined by a growing number of industry insiders, began to express a change of heart. And why not? During the first quarter of the year the number of insolvent thrifts declined—the first such decline in two years.[1] Moreover, around the time this positive statistic was unveiled, observers "discovered" something else of interest: although 1987 saw S & Ls lose over $6 billion nationwide, over two-thirds of all thrifts *made a profit* that year. In fact, profitable institutions earned, by year's end, about $6.6 billion.[2]

In assessing the uneven success of thrifts, James Barth, Bank Board chief economist, was blunt: "Clearly, the many are being pulled by the few."[3] He went on to reveal that twenty thrifts alone accounted for $2.1 billion in 1987 losses, and that these thrifts were located mainly in Texas and other states of the southwest. Furthermore, he pointed out, this geographical area represented 67 percent of the industry's losses.[4] So the problems frequently used to condemn an entire industry truly have been caused by a relatively few institutions.

Another sign of good health for the industry was evident after first-quarter statements were filed for 1988. Industry officials predicted that over 70 percent of all S & Ls nationwide should be profitable by the year's end.[5] And, as more and more weak thrifts merge with healthy ones, or undergo liquidation, this figure is very likely to rise steadily.

But perhaps the most encouraging S & L development of 1988, at least from the standpoint of those concerned about thrift consolidation (most notably the FHLBB), was the June announcement that MeraBank, a Phoenix, Arizona-based S & L, agreed to acquire thrifts in El Paso and Brownfield, Texas. Under the Southwest Plan, this was the first successful effort at recruiting out-of-state help for ailing S & Ls in Texas. In addition, this acquisition involved a substantial infusing of capital, which is precisely what the Board so desperately desired.[6]

Many, including FHLBB member Roger Martain, were greatly encouraged by this development. "They (MeraBank officials) are," Martain said, "demonstrating their faith in Texas." He further stated that "the significant fact is that we have an out-of-state institution that already has an operation in Texas, that has faith in Texas."[7] Indeed, Martain's optimism seems well-founded as MeraBank acquired a third institution in Texas in August 1988.

To be sure, the national S & L picture is improving measurably, and has been throughout 1988. With insolvent thrifts being merged or liquidated at a very rapid pace, and outside institutions almost certain to follow the lead of MeraBank (a proven winner among the nation's S & Ls), some observers continue to predict a collapse of the industry; but others feel the worst is over and the recovery has already begun. This is not to suggest that S & Ls are out of trouble—far from it, as of this writing. The cost estimates of the bail-out continue to grow each month, and currently range between $30 billion and $40 billion.[8] In the estimate of the authors, such figures are quite low now and, in the event of an economic downturn, will prove extremely low. In the authors' opinion, without a downturn in economic activity the final cost to the FHLBB and FSLIC to merge or liquidate weak and insolvent S & Ls should exceed $90 billion. The S & L industry will take center stage in the public's eye when the FHLBB finally admits that a taxpayer bail-out is inevitable. The increases in insurance premiums and sale of bonds by the federal insurance fund will not cover the problem loans that currently exist within the S & L industry. Once the funds are made available to merge or liquidate these problem institutions, the survival and future of the remaining healthy institutions looks good. But there should be no doubt about the nature of this "new" S & L industry. It is a far cry from the original, an industry that lasted for nearly one and one-half centures by fulfilling the American dream of home ownership. Today's thrifts also finance construction, real estate development, personal loans, and a host of other ventures. They do so by borrowing money not only via passbook accounts, but also through a variety of new types of certificates. Needless to say, increasingly complex institutions require increasingly complex solutions for their problems. Finding such solutions remains the challenge facing the modern S & L industry.

NOTES

1. Robert E. Taylor, "Insured Thrifts Post a Deficit of $3.78 Billion," *Wall Street Journal*, June 22, 1988, p. 7.

2. Maria Halkias, "Losing year for S & Ls," *The Dallas Morning News*, March 25, 1988, p. 1D.

3. *Ibid.*

4. *Ibid.*

5. Nathaniel C. Nash, "Bad numbers expected on S & L Industry," *The Dallas Morning News*, June 21, 1988, p. 8C.

6. Michael Weiss, "MeraBank to buy three Texas S & Ls," *The Dallas Morning News*, June 23, 1988, p. 1D.

7. *Ibid.*

8. *Ibid.*

Bibliography

BOOKS AND PAPERS

Bodfish, H. Morton (ed.). *History of Building and Loan in the United States*. Chicago: United States Building and Loan League, 1931.

Cagan, Phillip. *Peristent Inflation—Historical and Political Essays*. New York: Columbia University Press, 1979.

Carron, Andrew. *The Plight of Thrift Institutions*. Washington, D.C., 1982.

———. *The Rescue of the Thrift Industry*. Washington, D.C.: The Brookings Institution, 1983.

Cashin, Jack. "History of Savings and Loan Associations in Texas." Doctoral Dissertation, University of Texas, 1955.

Clark, Horace F. and Chase, Frank A. *Elements of the Modern Building and Loan Associations*. New York: Macmillan, 1925.

Donovan, John (ed.). *Democracy at the Crossroads*. New York: Holt, Rinehart, and Winston, 1978.

Edmister, Robert. *Financial Institutions: Markets and Management*. New York: McGraw-Hill, 1980.

Ewalt, Josephine. *A Business Reborn: The Savings and Loan Story, 1930–1960*. Chicago: American Savings and Loan Institute Press, 1962.

Hammond, Bray. *Banks and Politics in America: From the Revolution to the Civil War*. Princeton, N.J.: Princeton University Press, 1957.

Hoover, Robert. "The Behavioral Responses of Thrift Institutions to the Garn–St. Germain Depository Institutions Act of 1982." Master's Thesis, University of Texas, 1985.

Kendall, Leon T. *The Savings and Loan Business*. Englewood Cliffs, N.J.: Prentice-Hall, 1952.

Makinen, Gail. *Money, Banking and Economic Activity*. New York: Academic Press, 1981.

Marvell, Thomas B. *The Federal Home Loan Bank Board*. New York: Praeger, 1969, p. 36.

Pynn, Ronald E. *American Politics: Changing Expectations*. Monterey, Calif.: Brooks/Cole, 1984.

Ratner, Sidney; Soltow, James; and Sylla, Richard. *The Evolution of the American Economy*. New York: Basic Books, 1979.

Ritter, Lawrence and Silber, William. *Principles of Money, Banking, and Financial Markets*. New York: Basic Books, 1980.

Teck, Allan. *Mutual Savings Banks and Savings and Loan Associations: Aspects of Growth*. New York: Columbia University Press, 1968.

Williams, Edward. *Prospects for the Savings and Loan Industry to 1975*. Austin: Texas Savings and Loan League, 19 .

Woerheide, Walter J. *The Savings and Loan Industry: Current Problems and Possible Solutions*. Westport, Conn.: Quorum Books, 1984.

PERIODICALS, REPORTS, AND DOCUMENTS

"Banks, Thrifts Can Offer, Starting May 1, 91-day Certificates Paying Market Rates." *Wall Street Journal*. March 23, 1982, p. 2.

Binstein, Michael. "Feds detail cost of S & L bailout." *Austin American Statesman*, May 1, 1988, p. A1.

Brumbaugh, R. Dan, Jr. and Carron, Andrew. "Thrift Industry Crisis: Causes and Solutions." *Brookings Papers on Economic Activity*. Washington, D.C., 1987, p. 354.

Buckley, John M., Jr., "The Federal Home Loan Bank Board." *Federal Home Loan Bank Board Journal*. April 1982, p. 5.

Colton, Kent W. "Financial Reform: A Review of the Past and Prospects for the Future." Invited working paper no. 37, Office of Policy and Economic Research. Federal Home Loan Bank Board, September 1980, p. 15.

Crockett, John and King, Thomas. "The Contribution of New Asset Powers to S & L Earnings: A Comparison of Federal and State-Chartered Associations in Texas." *FHLBB Research Working Paper No. 110.* July 1982, p. 1.

"Deposit Insurance Reform Proposed." *Savings Bank Journal.* June 1983, p. 9.

Divers, William K. Statement, *Federal Home Loan Bank Board Journal.* April 1982, pp. 81–88.

Ewers, Joseph. "Current Commentary." *Texas League Savings Account.* Austin. November/December 1986, p. 12.

Federal Home Loan Bank Board News. Washington, D.C., May 13, 1988, p. 1.

FHLB-San Francisco Second Annual Conference: Change in The Savings and Loan Industry. San Francisco, 1976.

Fiftieth Annual Report of Texas Savings and Loan Associations. Texas Savings and Loan Department, Austin, 1978.

Fifty-Fourth Annual Report of Savings and Loan Associations. Texas Savings and Loan Department in cooperation with Texas Savings and Loan League, 1982.

A Financial Institution for the Future: Savings, Housing, Finance, Consumer Services: An Examination of the Restructuring of the Savings and Loan Industry. Washington, D.C.: Federal Home Loan Bank Board, 1975.

"Foreclosures spreading, report shows." *The Dallas Morning News.* June 14, 1988, p. 12D.

FSLIC–Insured Savings and Loan Associations Combined Financial Statements. Washington, D.C.: Federal Home Loan Bank Board, 1950, 1960, 1982.

"The Future Role of Thrift Institutions in Mortgage Lending." Proceedings of a conference on the Future of the Thrift Industry, October 1981. Boston: Federal Reserve Bank of Boston, 1981, p. 168.

General and Special Laws of the State of Texas, 41st Legislature, 2nd and 3rd Called Sessions, 1929. Austin: A. C. Baldwin and Sons, State Printers, 1929.

General and Special Laws of the State of Texas, 48th Legislature, Ch. 97, Subchapter I, Article 342–114, Vernon's Civil Statutes of the State of Texas. Austin, Texas.

General and Special Laws of the State of Texas, 57th Legislature, Chapter 198, Article 342–250, Vernon's Civil Statutes of the State of Texas. Austin, Texas.

General and Special Laws of the State of Texas, 58th Legislature, 1963, Article 852A, Vernon's Civil Statutes of the State of Texas. Austin, Texas.

Gray, Edwin. "Bank Board/Thrift Perspectives." *Federal Home Loan Bank Board Journal.* May/June 1983, p. 7.

————. "Matching Asset and Liabilities in a Thrift Portfolio." *Federal Home Loan Bank Board Journal.* September 1983, p. 3.

Guyon, Eugene, "A Critical Review of the Savings and Loan Industry." Professional Report, The University of Texas, 1983.

Halkias, Maria. "Losing year for S & Ls." *The Dallas Morning News.* March 25, 1988, p. 1D.

Hearing: Adequacy of FHLBB Supervision of Empire Savings and Loan Association. Committee on Government Operations, House of Representatives, 98th Congress, 2d session, April 25, 1984, p. 77.

Hilder, David B. and Taylor, Robert E., "Federal Regulators Liquidate 2 Thrifts in California for Record $1.35 Billion." *Wall Street Journal.* June 6, 1988, p. 2.

Home, John E. Statement, *Federal Home Loan Bank Board Journal.* April 1982, p. 79.

House Report: FHLBB Supervision and Failure of Empire Savings and Loan Association of Mesquite, Texas. Forty-fourth report by the Committee on Government Operations, August 6, 1984, p. 66.

Jaffee, Dwight M. "What to Do About Savings and Loan Associations?" *Journal of Money, Credit and Banking.* November 1974, p. 540.

Kane, Edward. "Deregulation, Savings and Loan Diversification and the Flow of Housing Finance." *Savings and Loan Asset Management Under Deregulation: Proceedings of the Sixth Annual Conference.* Federal Home Loan Bank of San Francisco, 1980.

Kupcke, Richard. "The Condition of Massachusetts Savings Banks and California Savings and Loan Associations." In *The Future of the Thrift Industry.* Boston: Federal Reserve Bank of Boston, 1981, p. 4.

Landendorf, Kirk. "Bank, S & L deposit rates worry officials." *Austin American Statesman.* February 21, 1988, p. H1.

————. "First half is brutal for S & Ls." *Austin American Statesman.* October 16, 1987, p. E1.

————. "S & L Regulators Running out of Time and Money." *Austin American Statesman.* September 14, 1986, p. J1.

————. "Ultimate wheeler-dealer." *Austin American Statesman.* June 5, 1988, p. D4.

"Landmark Garn–St. Germain in Legislation Becomes Law." *Savings Bank Journal*. November 1982, pp. 14–17.

Langley, Monica. "FSLIC's Reserves Dropped $1.1 Billion During 1985, According to GAO Audit." *Wall Street Journal*. July 3, 1986, p. 2.

Mahoney, Patrick, and White, Alice P. "The Thrift Industry in Transition." *Federal Reserve Bulletin*. Washington, D.C., March 1985, p. 1.

Martin, Preston. "New Credit Policies for the 1970s: A Discussion of FHLBB Objectives." *Federal Home Loan Bank Board Journal*. December 1970, p. 3.

McLean, Ken. "Legislative Background of the Depository Institutions Deregulation and Monetary Control Act of 1980." *Savings and Loan Asset Management Under Deregulation: Proceedings of the Sixth Annual Conference*. Federal Home Loan Bank of San Francisco, 1980, p. 23.

Nash, Nathaniel C., "Bad numbers expected on S & L Industry." *The Dallas Morning News*. June 21, 1988, p. 8C.

"Net Worth Requirements of Insured Institutions." *Federal Home Loan Bank Board Draft*. January 31, 1985, p. 1.

1986 Annual Report to Members: United States League of Savings Institutions. Chicago, 1986.

1986–1987 Texas Almanac. Dallas: A. H. Belo Corporation, 1986, p. 385.

1965 World Almanac and Book of Facts. New York: New York World Telegram, 1965.

"Officials express optimism over bond sale to aid FSLIC." *The Dallas Morning News*. October 1, 1987, p. 12D.

Pratt, Richard. "Office of the Chairman." *Federal Home Loan Bank Board— 1981 Annual Report*. April 1982, p. 6.

Pusey, Allen. "S & L: How they self-destructed." *The Dallas Morning News*. November 8, 1987, p. 1H.

"A Real Inflation Fighter Takes Charge at the Fed." *Fortune*. September 10, 1979, p. 62.

Richter, James L. "Office of the Federal Home Loan Banks." *Federal Home Loan Bank Board Journal*. April 1976, p. 25.

Ricks, R. Bruce and Friedman, Harris C. "The Housing Opportunity Allowance Program." *Federal Home Loan Bank Board Journal*. December 1971, p. 6.

Rules and Regulations for Texas Savings and Loan Associations. Promulgated and adopted November 15, 1963; August 30, 1965; July 14, 1967; August 3, 1973; September 15, 1974; July 16, 1979; March 3 & 31, 1981; October 28, 1981.

"Savings Accord to Help Banks, S & Ls is Cleared." *Wall Street Journal*. June 30, 1982.

"Savings Firms Face Problems From Land Loans—FBI Banking Investigators Are Reviewing Transactions." *Dallas Morning News*. December 5, 1983.

Savings Institutions Source Books. Chicago: United States League of Savings Institutions.

"S & Ls Show Their Political Punch." *Business Week*. November 23, 1981, p. 114.

Savings and Loan Fact Books. Chicago: United States Savings and Loan League.

"Savings and Loan Planning for the New Competitive Environment." *Federal Home Loan Bank Board Journal*. March/April 1981, p. 12.

Savings and Loan Source Books. Chicago: United States League of Savings Institutions.

Scheldhardt, Timothy D. "S & Ls Had Recorded $4.6 Billion Loss in 1981; $6 Billion Deficit Seen Possible This Year." *Wall Street Journal*. April 6, 1982.

"Some Glimmers of Hope." *Standard & Poor's Industry Surveys 1983*. Standard & Poor's Corporation, p. 827.

Taylor, Robert. "Bank Board Cooks Up Program Aimed at Speeding Up Disposal of Sick Thrifts." *Wall Street Journal*. June 17, 1988, p. 26.

———. "Bank Board Refusal to Shrink, S & L Levy Elicits Complaints from Thrift Industry." *Wall Street Journal*. April 4, 1988, p. 25.

———. "Bank Board Sharply Lifts Estimate on Costs of Ending Thrifts Crisis." *Wall Street Journal*. July 7, 1988, p. 3.

———. "FSLIC Deficit Nearly Doubled in 1987; Thrift Rescues Could Cost $15.3 Billion." *Wall Street Journal*. April 19, 1988, p. 10.

———. "Insured Thrifts Post a Deficit of $3.78 Billion." *Wall Street Journal*, June 22, 1988, p. 7.

———. "Thrifts' Struggle is Becoming Darwinian." *Wall Street Journal*. July 5, 1988, p. 6.

Texas Savings and Loan Directory. Texas Savings and Loan Department in cooperation with Texas Savings and Loan League, 1984–86.

U.S. Congress. *The Depository Institutions Deregulatory and Monetary Control Act of 1980*.

U.S. *Constitution*, Art. I, secs. 4 and 8.

Weiser, Charles M. "Texas Savings and Loan Branching." Professional Report. The University of Texas, December 1984, p. 1.

Weiss, Michael. "MeraBank to buy three Texas S & Ls." *The Dallas Morning News*. June 23, 1988, p. 1D.

————. "Thrifts Lose $3.8 billion." *The Dallas Morning News*. June 22, 1988, p. 1A.

West, Robert C. "The Depository Institutions Deregulation Act of 1980: A Historical Perspective." *Economic Review*. Federal Reserve Bank of Kansas City, February 1982, p. 3.

Wynter, Leon. "St. Germain Says House Won't Act to Aid FSLIC Without Plan From White House." *Wall Street Journal*. November 7, 1985, p. 6.

Yang, John, "Failed S & L Accounted for an Investment as Loan to Hide Loss, Bank Board Says," *Wall Street Journal*, September 15, 1986, p. 8.

Yang, John. "FSLIC Lacks Funds to Cover Loans to Thrifts." *Wall Street Journal*. January 22, 1986, p. 4.

Index

ABOUT THE AUTHORS

M. MANFRED FABRITIUS received his Ph.D. from the University of Texas at Austin and has taught business finance and economics at the college level for twelve years. Currently, he is an associate professor of economics at the University of Mary Hardin-Baylor in Belton, Texas. Previously, he has been on the faculties of New Mexico State University, Southwestern University, Southwest Texas State University, and the University of Texas at Austin.

WILLIAM BORGES received his Ph.D. from the University of California at Riverside and has taught political science for seven years. Presently, he is an assistant professor of political science at the University of Texas at Arlington.